PREFACE

The names of companies, directors and collection agents, lawyers have been changed in order to respect their anonymity.

In this 1st volume, you will enter the world of debt collection with its excesses and its leeway's but also on the side of debtors.

Lawyers quickly forgot their oath to impress their clients and the other side.

We don't encourage you to use the same techniques to get your bills paid.

We do not take sides either for debt collectors or for debtors.

The exchanges of emails between collectors and debtors are authentic.

Spelling errors were not corrected voluntarily.

The answers of both may seem repetitive because the commercial product is always the same.

Other volumes will be available soon.

Happy reading to all.

CASE N°1

Hello,

We never wanted to appear in any guide whatsoever, it was a usurpation and a fraudulent business, of which we never mandated anything. Also let me know that we will not pay these invoices which in fact are not the fruit of a dishonest and usurping enterprise of documents. The pursuit of your injunctions which have no value will never be taken into account because we have never, I repeat asked to appear in these so-called guides.

Mister X,

I thank you for your responsiveness.

Your attitude surprises me, I don't see anything fraudulent in this file, you have read and signed this order form, my client has provided the requested service.

The stamp affixed by your company on this purchase order commits you legally, it is quite normal that the invoices must be paid.

You write that my injunctions have no value:

-Is this the reason that my name is X?

You have to pay these bills.

Awaiting your response.

Regards,

Sir,

We will never pay an invoice! Because no request has been made from us! And believe me I am in my right, the scams you defend will not succeed! So you can continue your procrastination for a long time, we will no longer respond to any requests from you, we are not concerned!

Thank you for your understanding.

Hello Mister X,

You didn't bother to answer my last email of March 12, 2018.

Your silence will be prejudicial to you thereafter, the file is transferred to our legal service.
Try to negotiate this claim because after it will be impossible to do it with the bailiff.

Regards,

Mister X,

I understand your reaction but at the same time you must understand that I am in contact with you to help you find an amicable solution suitable for both parties.

This purchase order, which was filled out and then sent in a prepaid envelope for commercial purposes, I know you have not read it in full.

We all make mistakes like this and I know it's hard to admit that the error came from ourselves.

Let me insist in order to avoid you the future formal notice by bailiff, fees will be added.

At your request I can go to my Director of Cabinet, explain the situation to him and try to negotiate the claim (reduce the invoice).

I know that you are making it a matter of principle but it would be desirable for you to be less obstinate on this file, you will save time, energy and money.

I am waiting for your reply.

Greetings,

Mister X,

Hereby,

Having had no positive reaction from you.

I inform you and confirm that your file including the exchange of emails for unpaid invoices will be sent from Thursday, May 17, 2018 to the office of bailiffs to recover this claim with the consequences that this implies.

Greetings,

CASE N ° 2

Dear Sir

I am the board of the XYZ company organizing the ZZZ fair.

We have written twice to your principal, the company XYZ which by its actions causes confusion with our customers and thus performs acts of parasitic and deceptive unfair competition.

We also put him on notice to cease all steps with XYZ customers and any fraudulent attempt to contract with them through his well-known deceptive tactics.

It goes without saying that the company of M X will not settle the invoice obtained by deceitful maneuvers based on the confusion with our living room and on a service of your very doubtful client.

I therefore put you on notice to cease all requests against Mr. X and the other customers of the XYZ salon.

Best regards

COCO
Lawyer

Sir,

I learn today that you persist in sending formal notices to my customers without foundation. Worse, you lend yourself to acts of harassment that even threaten my clients over the phone.

You are aware that no claim is due unless it is disputed by an enforceable title, which you obviously do not present.

I put you on notice to immediately cease all new direct steps with Mr. X and XYZ.

If your company persists in its abusive claims, it must submit its claim to a French court. We will do our utmost to demonstrate on this occasion the fraudulent maneuvers undertaken.

My clients read me in copy.

I am available to your lawyer if you wish.

Greetings

Dear Y,

I don't see any harassment on my part, I do my collection work certainly hated but honest!

The fact that my name is Y does not give you the right to speak to me in this tone!

I never contact XYZ and never will, I have no records for this company!

Take the file and read the terms of the contract at the bottom of the page, it's a POPO contract not BILIBILI!

What fraudulent schemes are you talking about?

You are a lawyer and not a judge, stop defaming yourself.

Your formal notice is obsolete, I am not your employee.

I know that your customers read you a copy, needless to say.

Why do you want to speak with my lawyer?
Do you mind pursuing this file with me?

Does my first name bother you?

The file will go this month to the bailiff, Mr. X you refused my help for this file, the bailiff will ask you for the full invoice with additional fees.
You have until the end of March to contact me and settle this unpaid invoice.

Regards,

Dear X,

It is obvious that my mail is unequivocally addressed to your company and not to you personally.

M X will not pay you your invoice because he disputes it. No need to restart it.

We are therefore awaiting the summons before the court of JUPITER. Thank you for sending me a copy before delivery.

Finally it is in our ethical rules of the CORRUPTLAND bar that we seek the assistance of your counsel in a dispute.

cordially

Dear Y,

The fact that you have announced that you are counsel for Mr. X, I expect from you a power of attorney proving that you have all the powers for the company you represent. as I did on my side with Mister X.

Give me the opportunity to remind you of the following business rules:

The order signed by your client Mr. X has been received by my client the company XYZ, your client has contractual obligations.

I'm sorry to tell you that you forgot in your client's situation, the expenses could be tripled in case my client XYZ is the winner in court of MELI MELO.

I hope you have warned your client Mister X about these possible expenses.

When I receive your proxy regarding your official position on behalf of Mr. X's company we will be able to continue our conversation.

Cordialeement,

Dear Sir

A lawyer acting on behalf of his client does not have to justify a special power since he draws from articles 416 and 417 of the CPC a general representation mandate

 Internet link.

Furthermore, I am the only advisor to my clients, thank you for not advising them, which would amount to illegal canvassing.

For the rest of our discussions, I am your only contact, so I ask you to no longer copy my clients, Mr. X and XYZ

cordially

Hello Mister X,

At the request of my Director of Cabinet, please find attached the payment agreement / contract termination already signed by my client.

If you wish to settle this dispute amicably, all you have to do is sign it and send it back to me.

For bank transfer, in the subject of the payment, indicate only your file number (000000) so that our accounts can quickly identify your payment.

You have until the end of March to settle your bill, without any reaction from you, I inform you and confirm that your file will be sent to the office of bailiffs.

Contact details of the bailiff available at your request.

You can of course inform Z (Your lawyer) of my email. Cordialement,

Dear Sir

M X forwards your correspondence to me. It lets you know that your proposition is null and void and does not follow up on what could be assimilated to an extortion attempt.

Please send us the bailiff's contact details.

The file is closed on our side.

cordially

My dear,

I thank you for your email.

For starters, regarding your comments on "attempted extortion".
You write words that are quite harsh and I don't think you believe what you write because you don't really know the meaning of the words, you use these words just to impress Mr. X.

Here is the meaning of "attempted extortion":

Extortion is the act of obtaining, by violence, threat of violence or coercion, a signature, a commitment or a renunciation, or the revelation of a secret, or the handing over of funds, values or any other property.

I proposed to Mr. X to close this file with a payment agreement / contract termination and I have a shameful response from you.

You can close this file on your side but my duty is to inform you that you are destroying the amicable route of this file to the detriment of Mr. X.

Our principal XYZ will use all legal means to collect this claim including ancillary expenses.

Mister X, don't forget that you still have a few days to pay this bill, the bailiff will not accept any negotiations from you.

Mister X you must understand this:

- For a lawyer it is important that a case "drags on" because in parallel his fees increase.

It does not matter to him whether you are a winner or a loser because in the end he will have received his fees.

Regards,

Dear Sir

I see the debate shifting over the legal profession and am ready to discuss it with you.

As you know we are a profession regulated by law.

The same is true of collection companies like yours, so I would be grateful if you could send me a copy of the declaration of your activity to the Public Prosecutor allowing you to practice in the territory of CORRUPTLAND.

In the meantime.

Best regards

Hello Master,

According to the different directives of the European Union which regulate these fields, our company registered with URANUS, as member of the European Union, has no limits and without restriction of work with each government of the EU.

After that, in my first email, I presented our company as a collection agency including the document that we are mandated by XYZ.

Did Mr. X send you a document?
Here it is again!

I would like to ask you, are we going to close this file by mutual agreement, and save time and money for the 2 parties or we will have to proceed with an order for payment to which there will be a fairly substantial sum for Mr. X, accumulating interest for the last payment, accumulating taxes, also including your fees, on the side of your client.

I wait for your part, an enthusiastic response and I believe that you will be able to advise and inform Mister X the best way to close this affair.

Have a good weekend.

Regards,

Dear Sir

You have not sent me a copy of your declaration of activity to the Public Prosecutor, your company is therefore not authorized to exercise its recovery activity according to the legislation of CORRPUTLAND.

I again confirm that there is no amicable outcome to this matter.

Thank you for stopping to approach us.
cordially

Dear Z,

I take into consideration your refusal to settle this matter by mutual agreement.

Reading your statement about the authorization by the Prosecutor of the Republic of CORRUPTLAND, I ask you to check the directives of the European Union and to read carefully the information requested.

I'm still waiting for your written proof from you with the stamp of your study proving that you are indeed the counsel of Mr. X, the law requires you.

And finally I inform you that we will immediately take the first legal steps to collect this claim from Mr. X.

It would seem that you do not believe the future formal notice by bailiff.

My dear Z, you think of your fees at the expense of Mr. X, this is very unfortunate on your part.

Regards,

Mister X,

You have until March 30, 2018 to return this signed payment agreement to me, after it will be too late and the bailiff will ask you for the entire invoice to be paid with additional costs.

Now make your decision but do not be surprised when you receive the formal notice by bailiff, everything I told you will take effect and you will see that your lawyer has lied to you since the beginning of this case.

Regards,

Mister X,

Since the amicable confrontation with our Cabinet of judicial officers failed:

I would like to inform you that our client XYZ. will sue you on URANUS in the court of JUPITER to assert its rights.

The amount claimed will be 3 years 4000, 00 EUROS + recovery costs) as written on the contract that you have read and signed.

We are required to inform you that this legal action does not require the legal consent or the presence of your company and that the case will be decided solely on the basis of the evidence provided by the claimant which gives rise to a payment mandate. by default. The judgment will be executed in accordance with international regulations to which your country is also bound, in particular the international convention on the recognition and enforcement of foreign judgments in civil and commercial matters and the international convention on choice of court agreements.

We are also required to inform you that on the basis of similar international conflicts, we can estimate your final disbursement, including late fees, court fees and legal fees, between Euro 12,000.00 and Euro 15,000.00.

I keep your file until September 24, 2018.

Regards,

CASE N° 3

Dear Mr. X,

On March 13, 2018, I sent you the file by email regarding this unpaid invoice.

You read my email the same day but no response from you.

Should I conclude from this that you refuse to pay this invoice or else my first name causes you communication problems?

I am waiting for a response from you as soon as possible.

Regards,

Mr.

I hardly appreciate your hints about your name. I ask you a minimum of respect!

Then, I did not follow up on your first email because we are currently in contact with our law firm as well as the fraud enforcement services which are studying this matter closely.
So we are awaiting the results of a little further analysis of these 2 services, but I can already tell you that you will soon have news.

Cordially.

Dear Mr. X,

I thank you for your responsiveness.

The minimum of respect I think is to respond to each email as soon as possible.

You tell me about the XYZ, once again I think you associate my origins with fraud.

Since this is so, I will in turn also contact 2 organizations that you have in CORRUPTLAND fighting against racism.

Does that suit you ???

For the record, this purchase order, you signed it with the stamp of the company, then sent in a pre-paid envelope for commercial purposes.

My client has honored his service since 2016:

Internet link

The invoices have not been paid!
And after you don't respond to my email, you bring up the XYZ to try not to pay these bills.
Have you forgotten your obligations as a business manager, Mr. X?!?

I keep your file until the end of this week and without payment from you, the file will be sent to the office of the bailiff.

And for information it is a tacit renewal contract.

Regards,

Mr.

I don't like your tone at all. I have no lessons to receive from you!

Dear Mr. X,

I am still awaiting payment from you.

We have this week to close this file amicably, in case of failure your file will go to the bailiff and fees will be added.

By signing this order form, you have legally committed yourself, my client has carried out active advertising since 2016:

Internet link.

If you signed this purchase order without having read it in full, it is your fault, my client is not responsible for your negligence.

I can of course help you to close this dispute amicably and even negotiate this claim with my Chief of Staff if you wish.

I look forward to hearing from you as soon as possible.

Regards,

Hello Mrs. Y,

Thank you for your answer.

Why does Mister X refuse to pursue this file with me?

Again it seems obvious that my first name Z bothers him!
How should I take this attitude?

So I would like to know if Mr. X wishes to find an amicable solution to close this file!

Regards,

Sir,

Mr X as Director of our company has many other things to do than manage this kind of file and whatever the name of his interlocutor. This debate is closed.
Our legal department will come back to you if necessary.

Cordially.

Mr.
I can no longer accept these allusions and I take this for a personal attack.
Do I have to tell you that I am gay and that my partner is called Z?
I expect an apology from you otherwise it is I who will file a complaint against you!

Mister X,

Your privacy does not interest me!
No personal attack on my part but your professional position does not allow you to answer me with a haughty air, nothing more.

I am in contact with you to close this file by mutual agreement.

The current problem is that you do not assume that you have signed a purchase order without having read it in full !!!!!!!!!!!!!!
I understand you and put myself in your place in such circumstances, we all have our pride and so do I.

We all make mistakes, including myself.

Can you put your pride aside for this file?
I'll do the same on my side.

Who has read a bank or insurance contract in full before signing it ???
So I ask you again these last questions:

Do you want YES or NO to close this file by mutual agreement ???

Do you want YES or NO to negotiate this claim for you with my Director of Cabinet?

A payment agreement / contract termination will be established at your request!

Please answer these questions and I won't bother you anymore!

If you refuse my help, I will respect your choice but your file will go to the bailiff.

Regards,

CASE N° 4

Dear Sir,

I have forwarded your file, which is nothing more than an attempted scam, to my Council, Maître Z, in copy of this email.

I will take stock with him soon regarding identity theft and falsification of documents.

For the time being, if however an impostor came to present itself on our premises, we will inform the gendarmerie services within a minute.

You are well informed.

cordially

Dear Mr. X,

But what scam are you talking about?

As you can see, the stamp of your company is legally binding on this order form.

My Client XYZ has carried out the advertising service for which you have subscribed.

You can file a complaint, this will not erase the claim since the commercial is dissociated from the criminal.

I note that you have associated my first name with scam.

We have this week to close this claim out of court.

Greetings.

Dear Sir,

I dispute your claim.

cordially

Mister X,

You have the right to dispute this claim but you also have your obligations as a business manager:

- settle your invoices
-to assume your responsibilities

Your file will be sent to the bailiff next Monday if you do not pay this claim.

Regards,

Mister X,

I would like to inform you that your file will be sent from Tuesday, March 20, 2018 to our office of bailiffs to recover this claim with the consequences that this entails (Order to pay, attachment to bank account, entry in the debtors register).

The amount claimed by the bailiff will be 5,000, 00 EUROS (+ costs).

Being the mediator between you and my client for this file, I remain at your disposal.

Greetings,

CASE N° 5

Hello Z,

Are you aware of these invoices? If not, can you send the file to the replacement for Y stp?

Thank you in advance for your help.

Best Regards, Best Regards

Hello X,

No one is aware of this command. This supplier does not even exist with us. I find out what we can do and keep you posted.

Regards,

Mrs. X,

My colleague ZY sent you by email on March 06, 2018 a file concerning an unpaid invoice.

No positive reaction from you.

I would like to inform you that your file will be sent from Friday, March 30, 2018 to our office of bailiffs to recover this claim with the consequences that this entails (order to pay, attachment to bank account, entry in the debtors register).

The amount claimed by the bailiff will be 2,519.35 EUROS (+ costs).

Being the mediator between you and my client for this file, I remain at your disposal.

cordially

Hello Mrs. X,

I have not received any news from you for this unpaid invoice (File sent by email on March 06, 2018).

At the request of my client, I ask you one last time to settle this claim!

I am the mediator between you and my client.

If we do not find an amicable solution this week, your file will be sent to the office of bailiffs early next week.

Maybe you prefer to settle these invoices directly to the bailiff ???

Regards,

Hello,
We responded to your reminders by this letter in attachment.
No further action will be taken by XYZ on this matter, and if you continue to contact us in this way, we will file a complaint with the competent authorities.
Cordially

CASE N°6

Hello sir

You forgot to send me the advertisement from the referenced newspaper

cordially

Dear Sir,

Here again is the link on the active advertising service since 2016:

Internet link

Regards,

Dear Mr. X,

On March 13, 2018, I sent you an email with the file regarding this unpaid invoice.

You read my email the same day but no response from you.

I am waiting for a response from you as soon as possible.

Regards,

Hello sir

I call you before Wednesday

cordially

Hello sir

I inform you that you will receive a Recommended

cordially

Dear Mr. X,

This answer is far from clear.

Please inform your Direction as soon as possible that this file will be transmitted from Monday, March 26, 2018 to the office of bailiffs to recover this claim.

Regards,

Sir,

The terms of your email cannot impress my client, the company XYZ, and I assure you that I do not need a license to file a complaint in the hands of the Public Prosecutor.

I confirm that you have also contacted the services of ABCD.

Best regards

NB: thank you kindly acknowledge receipt of this shipment by a simple AR by return email.

My dear,

It seems that you associate my first name YZ with something criminal!

But why then file a complaint?
So as not to pay bills?
Frankly a little serious my dear Y!

You can enter all the organizations you want:

- My work is certainly hated but honest.

And aren't the terms you use in this email intimidating?

I, in turn, may file a complaint with the President of the Bar in your city because this letter is contrary to article 8 of the national internal regulations.

What do you think ?

With your excessive ego, you have forgotten that you are like me and like everyone else, a human being nothing more!

Your years of study to learn more or less by heart different codes (civil, criminal, etc. etc.) do not give you the right to speak to me in this tone.

And I find you very ungrateful to me, because thanks to me with this file, I save you money.

These invoices must be paid and they will be paid.

CASE N°7

Hello,

Since neither you nor your client have a CORRUPTLAND telephone number, please contact me to discuss it verbally.

Regards,

Mrs. Z,

After hearing from my Director of Cabinet, I was able to reduce this debt to you.

Please find attached the payment agreement / termination of contract to return to me signed with the stamp of the company if you wish to close this file by mutual agreement.

For the purpose of the payment, indicate only the file number so that our accounts can quickly identify the payment:

000000

If you refuse, it is your right and I respect it, in this case I will be forced to send your file to our office of bailiffs to recover this claim with the consequences that this implies.

Greetings.

Mrs. Y,

Since the amicable confrontation with our Cabinet of judicial officers failed:

I would like to inform you that our client XYZ. will sue you on SATURNE in the court of JUPITER to assert its rights.

The amount claimed will be 3 years (4000, 00 EUROS + recovery costs) as written on the contract that you have read and signed.

We are required to inform you that this legal action does not require the legal consent or the presence of your company and that the case will be decided solely on the basis of the evidence provided by the claimant which gives rise to a payment mandate. by default. The judgment will be executed in accordance with international regulations to which your country is also bound, in particular the international convention on the recognition and enforcement of foreign judgments in civil and commercial matters and the international convention on choice of court agreements.

We are also required to inform you that on the basis of similar international conflicts, we can estimate your final disbursement, including late fees, court fees and legal fees, between Euro 12,000.00 and Euro 15,000.00.

I keep your file until September 24, 2018.

Regards,

Hello sir,

Do you have the possibility to contact me by phone?

I would like to remind you that the person who signed the contract (contract of which we were only aware during your intervention on the file on April 19, 2018, because on the invoices we received, we could not contact anyone in France and thought it was a scam to get us settled) had no power. In addition, the stamp affixed does not contain our TAX ID number, nor any other legal information. It is only a commercial stamp.
The only person who can commit our company is the president.
Also in CORRUPTLAND law, if the signatory does not have the power to sign, the contract lapses.

Hello Mrs. Z,

It does not matter who signed this order because the company is responsible for its employees.

And to leave the stamp of society visible and available to everyone is a serious professional error.

Let me remind you of these facts:

This order form with cover letter was sent by publi postage (postal mail).

This purchase order was read, then signed and returned in a pre-paid envelope for commercial purposes.

Madam Z, as far as I know, the person acted of his own free will, no one forced him, sorry to write this but the fault lies with him, my client is not responsible for this negligence.

The cover letter clearly explained the commercial offer, the person should have read the entire letter and the order form.

And since 2015 my client has honored the requested advertising service:

Internet link.

My Cabinet Director offers you one last chance to settle this claim.

If you refuse, it is your right and I respect it, in this case the company XYZ will be assigned to the court of JUPITER with the consequences set out in my previous email.

Please find enclosed the payment agreement / termination of contract to return to me signed with the stamp of your company if you wish to close this file by mutual agreement.

Once signed, I will send it to my client who will do the same and I will return it to you.

In the subject of the settlement put only the file number so that our accounting department can quickly identify the payment:

000000

Do not forget to send me proof of the transfer made.

Regards,

Mister X,

We fully understand your position.
The stamp affixed is a simple commercial stamp and does not present any legal information.
Again, in CORRUPTLAND, a contract is only valid if it is signed by a person authorized and authorized to commit the company. This is not the case here.

However, I will present your mail to the manager and will be sure to get back to you early next week.

CASE N°8

Hello,

Thank you for sending me your email exchanges and order form signed by our contact please!

Waiting to read you

Hello Madam,

You already have the order form sent in my previous email, the contact person is Ms. Z, it is listed on the order form.

Regards,

Hello Mrs. Y,

I thank you for your responsiveness.

The service provided has been visible here on this link since 2016:

Internet link.

For the record, this order form was read and signed with the stamp of the company, then this order form was sent in a pre-franked envelope for commercial purposes.

The signature as well as the stamp of the company binds you legally, the invoices must be paid.

What scam are you talking about?

Are you associating my First Name Y with a scam ???

I can in my turn, send this file (including your email) to various organizations that you have in CORRUPTLAND which fight against racism.

You can file a complaint, this will not erase the claim since the salesperson is dissociated from the criminal.

And legally, it does not matter who signed this order because the company is responsible for its employees.

We have until the end of March to close this file amicably and find a suitable solution for both parties (you and my client).

Awaiting your response for a possible proposal from you.

Regards,

We have communicated your contact details to the authorities to find you! You author of this scam!

Mrs. Z,

I have not received any news from you for this unpaid invoice (File sent by email on March 07, 2018).

You have read my emails and you persist in your silence, this attitude shows that you are guilty and without valid arguments on this matter.

At the request of my client, I ask you one last time to settle this claim!

I am the mediator between you and my client.

If we do not find an amicable solution this week, your file will be sent to the office of bailiffs early next week.

Regards,

Mrs. Z,

ASSUME WHAT YOU SIGNED !!!

AND ESPECIALLY READ A DOCUMENT IN FULL BEFORE SIGNING AND RETURNING IT.

You must understand that you are solely responsible for this situation, no one forced you to fill out this order form and then return it in a pre-paid envelope for commercial purposes.

Today you are in conflict with yourself through your own neglect.

If you prefer to pay directly to the bailiff I give you his contact details as well as a new payment agreement / contract termination.

Regards,

CASE N°9

Hello,

These bills have never been posted on our side. After checking, we see that this is a scam.
We will therefore be forced to file a complaint for a scam against XYZ.

Regards,

Y
Accounting

Hello Mrs. Z,

I thank you for your responsiveness.

The service provided has been visible here on this link since 2016:

Internet link

For the record, this order form was read and signed with the stamp of the company, then this order form was sent in a pre-franked envelope for commercial purposes.

The signature as well as the stamp of the company binds you legally, the invoices must be paid.

What scam are you talking about?

Are you associating my First Name X with a scam ???

I can in my turn, send this file (including your email) to various organizations that you have in CORRUPTLAND which fight against racism.

You can file a complaint, this will not erase the claim since the salesperson is dissociated from the criminal.

Be kind to do a survey within your company to find out who signed this purchase order!

And legally, it does not matter who signed this order because the company is responsible for its employees.

We have until the end of March to close this file amicably and find a suitable solution for both parties (you and my client).

Awaiting your response for a possible proposal from you.

Regards,

Hello,

Absolutely not.

I see with my CEO early next week and come back to you.

Regards,

Y
Accounting

Dear,

My colleague X sent you by email on March 07, 2018 a file concerning an unpaid invoice.

No positive reaction from you.

I would like to inform you that your file will be sent from Friday, March 30, 2018 to our office of bailiffs to recover this claim with the consequences that this entails (order to pay, attachment to bank account, entry in the debtors register).

The amount claimed by the bailiff will be 4,000.00 EUROS (+ costs).

Being the mediator between you and my client for this file, I remain at your disposal.

Regards,

Hello,

These bills have never been posted on our side. After checking, we see that this is a scam.
We will therefore be forced to file a complaint for a scam against XYZ.

Remaining at your disposal,

Regards,

Mrs. Y,

No positive reaction from you for this unpaid invoice.
I would like to inform you that your file will be sent from Monday, April 16, 2018 to our office of bailiffs to recover this claim with the consequences that this entails (Order to pay, attachment to bank account, entry in the debtors register).

The amount claimed by the bailiff will be 4,000.00 EUROS (+ costs).

Contact details of the judicial officers available at your request.

Being the mediator between you and my client for this file, I remain at your disposal for a possible proposal from you.

Regards,

Mrs. Y,

Hereby,

Having had no positive reaction from you.

I inform you and confirm that your file including the exchange of emails for unpaid invoices will be transmitted from Wednesday May 16, 2018 to the office of bailiffs to recover this claim with the consequences that this implies.

Greetings

Mrs. Y,

I have not received any news from you for this unpaid invoice (File sent by email on March 07, 2018).

You have read my emails and you persist in your silence, this attitude shows that you are guilty and without valid arguments on this matter.

You have abused the trust of my client by not respecting the contract that you have read and signed.

At the request of my client, I ask you one last time to settle this claim!

I am the mediator between you and my client.

If we do not find an amicable solution this week, your file will be sent to the office of bailiffs early next week.

Maybe you prefer to settle these invoices directly to the bailiff ???

Failure to pay this amount within the stipulated time will immediately result in necessary legal action against your business for the original amount plus interest, collection costs, court fees, attorney fees and expenses. In accordance with the terms of the contract, the competent court is the Court of Justice of JUPITER, the applicable law is that of VENUS.

We are required to inform you that this legal action does not require the legal consent or the presence of your company and that the case will be decided solely on the basis of the evidence provided by the claimant which gives rise to a payment mandate. by default. The judgment will be executed in accordance with international regulations to which your country is also bound, in particular the international convention on the recognition and enforcement of foreign judgments in civil and commercial matters and the international convention on choice of court agreements.

We are also required to inform you that on the basis of similar international conflicts, we can estimate your final disbursement, including late fees, court fees and legal fees, between Euro 12,000.00 and Euro 15,000.00.

Regards,

Mrs. Y,

PAY YOUR INVOICES !!!

If you prefer to pay directly to the bailiff I give you his contact details as well as a payment agreement / contract termination.

Regards,

CASE N°10

Hello M.Z

We take note of your request.
That said, unless we are mistaken, we have not subscribed to a registration request on the site concerned.
The order form which is in the appendix seems strange to us, especially concerning the stamp used: XYZ is not located at 10, rue de laoule pas fraiche.
Furthermore, we do not see on this document the name of the signatory.

We remain at your disposal for any information
cordially
Mister X
Sales Manager

Hello Mister X,

I thank you for your responsiveness.

Regarding the stamp that was used, this does not concern me, it is a problem that concerns only the company XYZ.

This purchase order was sent by my customer by post, this purchase order was signed by a person within the company XYZ then this purchase order was returned in a stamped envelope letter T which as you know is for commercial purposes.

Can we find an amicable solution to close this file?

Regards,

Hello Mister X,

I did not receive a response to my last email!

Without communication from you, it will be difficult to close this file by mutual agreement.

I keep your file until Thursday March 15, 2018.

Regards,

Mister Z,
I just had a conversation with Mr. X regarding this claim.
For him, the signature on the order form is an imitation or fraudulent use of Mr. ZY's signature.
On the other hand, XYZ has never had its headquarters in FUNNYLAND, as the stamp at the bottom of the order form suggests:

XYZ is currently based on boulevard ROTOTO 235 00000 VAOPO. It was previously domiciled at rue du PETIT MULET 00000 CHIPAOLI.

It was never based in FUNNYLAND on rue du JOLI BLAIREAU 0000 TAITOI.

Consequently, having never dealt with a company whose name does not appear on its invoices (we assume that the name on the order form (POUPOU…?) Is the name of this company), we strongly suspect these complaints as fraudulent attempts to extort money from us.

We leave you, Mr. Z, any latitude to transmit this file to the competent bailiff office, being confident in our good law and being able to prove it easily by the remarks enacted above.
Cordially .

Hello Mister YY,

But what fraud are you talking about?

Do you associate my first name Z with fraud?

On this purchase order, I see the signature of the Director, the stamp of the company, my client XYZ honored the advertising service that you ordered, it is quite normal that my client claims its due.

You mention a concern with the stamp, it remains an internal problem of your company.

This purchase order was sent in a stamped letter T envelope (for commercial purposes) to my client.

POUPOU means "received" in TERRILAND!

Your signature and the company stamp legally bind you.

You have to pay these bills!

Regards,

CASE N°11

Sir,

We have received this previously completed document asking us to confirm the accuracy of the information on this document. What we have done.

When we received your reminder of an invoice to be paid, we checked with the organization XYZ, which confirmed to us that it was the subject of a scam.

In the event that we receive an order to be paid by a bailiff, we will dispute and start a procedure for fraud against you.

The management is at your disposal for further information.

Greetings

Hello Mrs. Z,

I thank you for your responsiveness.

For the record, this order form has been read and signed, then sent in a prepaid envelope for commercial purposes.

The signature commits you legally, the invoices must be paid.

My client XYZ is not responsible if Mr. X signed this purchase order without having read it in full, the fault lies with him.

What scam are you talking about?

If I understand correctly XYZ told you not to pay your bills:

- Incitement to crime ……… .. punishable as a crime.

Are you associating my First Name Y with a scam ???

I can in my turn, send this file (including your letter) to various organizations that you have in CORRUPTLAND which fight against racism.

You can file a complaint, this will not erase the claim since the salesperson is dissociated from the criminal.

We have this week to close this file amicably and find a suitable solution for both parties (you and my client).

And I inform you and confirm that your file will go to the bailiff to collect this claim if no amicable solution is not possible.

I do a hated but honest job.

Awaiting your response for a possible proposal from you.

Regards,

Mrs. Z,

My colleague Y sent you by email on March 14, 2018 a file concerning an unpaid invoice.

You read this email with the file on March 14, 2018 and unfortunately no reaction from you.

I would like to inform you that your file will be sent from Monday, March 26, 2018 to our office of bailiffs to recover this claim with the consequences that this entails (Order to pay, attachment to bank account, entry in the debtors register).

The amount claimed by the bailiff will be 5,000, 00 EUROS (+ costs).

Being the mediator between you and my client for this file, I remain at your disposal.

Regards,

Mrs. Z,

Hereby,

I inform you and confirm that your file for unpaid invoice has been sent to the office of bailiffs to recover this claim with the consequences that this implies.

Greetings.

CASE N°12

Mister X,

PAY YOUR INVOICES !!!

If you prefer to pay directly to the bailiff I give you his contact details as well as a payment agreement / contract termination.

Regards,

Mr.
Write me again and I will complain to the police

Mister X,

Your threats don't impress me!

Are you associating my origins with something illegal?

If you continue in this direction, I will not hesitate to contact 2 organizations that you have in CORRUPTLAND like ABCD or the EFGH and to file a complaint against you for discrimination in name and surname.

You want to file a complaint with the Police!
What is the purpose of not paying your bills?

Since 2016 my client has honored his advertising service:

Internet link.

YOU MUST ASSUME WHAT YOU SIGN AND RESPECT YOUR CONTRACTUAL OBLIGATIONS.

I am in contact with you to close this file by mutual agreement, so I ask you a little serious.

I do a hated but honest job.

In short the criminal being dissociated from the commercial, this will not erase the invoices.
And after 30 days, the file will be closed without further action.

By filing a complaint for X reasons, you will be making a false statement.

If you are making a complaint, please be so kind as to send me a copy so that I can add it to your file.

So if you refuse to settle these invoices out of court, I will send your file to the bailiff in order to collect this claim.

And if you have complained to the Police or the Gendarmerie, you will be prosecuted for false declaration, the bailiff is a ministerial officer and will not give you any gifts.

If you prefer to pay directly to the bailiff I give you his contact details as well as a payment agreement / contract termination.

Regards,

CASE N°13

Dear,

My colleague Mohamed X sent you by email on March 06, 2018 a file concerning an unpaid invoice.

No positive reaction from you.

I would like to inform you that your file will be sent from Friday, March 30, 2018 to our office of bailiffs to recover this claim with the consequences that this entails (order to pay, attachment to bank account, entry in the debtors register).

The amount claimed by the bailiff will be 3,000.00 EUROS (+ costs).

Being the mediator between you and my client for this file, I remain at your disposal.

Regards,

Hello Mister Z,

I would like to get in touch with you regarding the dispute mentioned below.

This is an invoice from March 11, 2016 received to which we replied by official mail on two grounds of non-admissibility of the invoice and therefore termination:

    * this invoice was never the subject of a request or an order on the part of XYZ but of the supplement of a questionnaire on an exhibition of exhibition by a person not legally authorized to engage the company XYZ;

    * no service was performed either in 2016 or in 2017

In this sense, I would therefore like to exchange with you before being pushed to initiate a legal action on the basis of your email below which provides for the call to a bailiff.

Regards,

Hello Mister Y,

I thank you for your responsiveness.

The service provided has been visible here on this link since 2016:

Internet link

For the record, this order form was read and signed with the stamp of the company, then sent in a pre-paid envelope for commercial purposes (see attachment).

The signature as well as the stamp of the company binds you legally, the invoices must be paid.

It does not matter who signed this purchase order since the company is responsible for its employees.

By re-reading the terms of the contract at the bottom of the page, it is written that the contract termination letter had to arrive 12 days after the date written on the order form.

Your letter arrived far too late.

The fault lies with the company XYZ, the stamp of the company should not be made available to anyone.

We have this week to close this file amicably and find a suitable solution for both parties (you and my client).

A payment / contract termination agreement will be established at your request if you wish to close this file by mutual agreement.

Awaiting your response for a possible proposal from you.

Regards,

Thanks for your feedback.

I can offer you a telephone meeting either Tuesday 27/03 morning (at your convenience for the time), or Wednesday 28/03 between 11h and 12h.

cordially

Hello Mister Y,

Sorry to answer you late but I am overwhelmed by several quite important files which must also be closed like yours at the end of this week.

And I will be in a meeting almost every day during this week.

Do you have a proposal to make to me to find a favorable outcome to this file?

I remain of course open to any negotiation on your part.

Greetings,

Hello Mr. Z,

given that we had denounced by mail as soon as the questionnaire was completed but that the service was carried out, I can offer you to settle the first invoice only.

I consider that the second year of service did not need to be given our letter of dispute and request for cancellation of this engagement not validated by an authorized person.

Thank you in advance for your feedback on this proposal.

Regards,

Hello Mister Y,

Thank you for your answer.

I will go to my Director of Cabinet and tell him about your proposal.

At the end of the morning I come back to you.

Greetings.

Hello Mister Y,

After hearing from my Director of Cabinet, I was able to reduce this debt to you.

Please find attached the payment agreement / termination of contract to return to me signed with the stamp of the company if you wish to close this file by mutual agreement.

In the subject of the payment, indicate only the file number so that our accounting department can quickly identify your payment:

000000

Also send me the proof of payment so that I can block your file and avoid the crumbs by bailiff.

Greetings.

Hello Mr. Z,

I take note of this agreement and I confirm the payment on my side.

The invoice will be paid with the transfer wave of 30 so I would be able to send you the proof of payment Tuesday or Wednesday.

Regards,

Hello Mister Y,

I thank you for your responsiveness.

Do not forget to return the signed agreement to me so that I can send it to my client for him to sign.

Greetings.

Hello,

I take note of your request.

However, we are regularly subject to fraudulent payment attacks and I cannot validate a payment under these conditions.

XYZ must first sign the payment agreement document and I can speak to them orally in order to perform certain checks.

Our internal procedure is very strict on this checkpoint and no payment can be validated without meeting these conditions.

In the present case I insist all the more on this subject given the bank details transmitted.

Regards,

Hello Mister Y,

Yes of course,

I transmit this payment agreement to my client so that he signs it and returns it to you by email upon receipt.

Regards,

Hello Mister Y,

Attached is the document signed by my client.

Regards,

Hello M.Z,

attached the countersigned document.

The transfer returned invalidated by the bank on the grounds that the beneficiary's bank details are incorrect.

Could you confirm them?

Thanks in advance.

Regards,

Hello Mister Y,

Attached again the RIB in attached file.

We have no problem with this bank account.

Once the payment is made, can you send me the SWIFT document from the bank?

Regards,

CASE N°14

Hello sir,

Our company did not place an order with XYZ (neither in 2016 nor in 2017).
XYZ is not listed in our supplier database and you are unable to provide me with an order number via our procedure.
No payment will be made on these items provided.

Good reception,
Cordially.

Mrs,

Your internal order number procedure is just a pretext for not paying invoices.

This fraudulent system is well known in CORRUPTLAND.

I will send your file to the bailiff tomorrow morning to collect this claim with the consequences that this implies.

Regards,

Mrs. Y,

My colleague X sent you by email on March 14, 2018 a file concerning an unpaid invoice.

You read this email with the file on March 14, 2018 and unfortunately no reaction from you.

I would like to inform you that your file will be sent from Monday, March 26, 2018 to our office of bailiffs to recover this claim with the consequences that this entails (Order to pay, attachment to bank account, entry in the debtors register).

The amount claimed by the bailiff will be 3,000.00 EUROS (+ costs).

Being the mediator between you and my client for this file, I remain at your disposal.

Regards,

Hello

Please send me OUR order number without which I cannot save the invoice

Waiting to read you

cordially

Hello Mrs. Y,

I thank you for your responsiveness.

The only order number I have in my possession is:

000000

I send you the order form, as well as the invoices.

Regards,

Mr.

I'm sorry but this is not an order from us

cordially

Dear,

I have not received any news from you for this unpaid invoice (File sent by email on March 14, 2018).

You have read my emails and you persist in your silence, this attitude shows that you are guilty and without valid arguments on this matter.

At the request of my client, I ask you one last time to settle this claim!

I am the mediator between you and my client.

If we do not find an amicable solution this week, your file will be sent to the office of bailiffs early next week.

Maybe you prefer to settle these invoices directly to the bailiff ???

Failure to pay this amount within the stipulated time will immediately result in necessary legal action against your business for the original amount plus interest, collection costs, court fees, attorney fees and expenses. In accordance with the terms of the contract, the competent court is the Court of Justice of JUPITER, the applicable law is that of VENUS.

We are required to inform you that this legal action does not require the legal consent or the presence of your company and that the case will be decided solely on the basis of the evidence provided by the claimant which gives rise to a payment mandate. by default. The judgment will be executed in accordance with international regulations to which your country is also bound, in particular the international convention on the recognition and enforcement of foreign judgments in civil and commercial matters and the international convention on choice of court agreements.

We are also required to inform you that on the basis of similar international conflicts, we can estimate your final disbursement, including late fees, court fees and legal fees, between Euro 12,000.00 and Euro 15,000.00.

Regards,

CAS N°15

Mrs. Z,

I'm still waiting for a response from you for these unpaid invoices.

Regards,

Hello,

The file has been sent to our legal department.

I am awaiting their return. I would therefore be grateful if you would give us a few more days to give them time to study the matter.

Regards,

Mrs. Z,

No more news since June 26, 2018.

I inform you that the file will be sent to the bailiff on Wednesday July 4, 2018 to recover this claim.

Regards,

Dear,

My colleague X sent you by email on March 15, 2018 a file concerning an unpaid invoice.

No positive reaction from you.

I would like to inform you that your file will be sent from Friday, March 30, 2018 to our office of bailiffs to recover this claim with the consequences that this entails (order to pay, attachment to bank account, entry in the debtors register).

The amount claimed by the bailiff will be 3,000.00 EUROS (+ costs).

Being the mediator between you and my client for this file, I remain at your disposal.

Regards,

Dear,

I have not received any news from you for this unpaid invoice (File sent by email on March 15, 2018).

You have read my emails and you persist in your silence, this attitude shows that you are guilty and without valid arguments on this matter.

You have abused the trust of my client by not respecting the contract that you have read and signed.

At the request of my client, I ask you one last time to settle this claim!

I am the mediator between you and my client.

If we do not find an amicable solution this week, your file will be sent to the office of bailiffs early next week.

Maybe you prefer to settle these invoices directly to the bailiff ???

Failure to pay this amount within the stipulated time will immediately result in necessary legal action against your business for the original amount plus interest, collection costs, court fees, attorney fees and expenses. In accordance with the terms of the contract, the competent court is the Court of Justice of JUPITER, the applicable law is that of VENUS.

We are required to inform you that this legal action does not require the legal consent or the presence of your company and that the case will be decided solely on the basis of the evidence provided by the claimant which gives rise to a payment mandate. by default. The judgment will be executed in accordance with international regulations to which your country is also bound, in particular the international convention on the recognition and enforcement of foreign judgments in civil and commercial matters and the international convention on choice of court agreements.

We are also required to inform you that on the basis of similar international conflicts, we can estimate your final disbursement, including late fees, court fees and legal fees, between Euro 12,000.00 and Euro 15,000.00.

Regards,

Sir,

Your comments are completely inappropriate and show that your client only showed you what they were interested in.

Your client is hiding behind international events to promote a so-called advertising site.

The document is contentious because it highlights our participation in the XYZ trade show by implying that a registration has already been published.
Et comme je l'ai précédemment fait remarquer, je ne suis pas habilitée à signer des factures engageant la société à titre financier.

I asked to stop this insertion but your client has turned a deaf ear and is hiding behind a so-called commitment that has no value and thus makes forcing.

Your customer is being dishonest because he uses the name of international trade shows to make companies believe that this is just an update. These business methods are completely questionable and shameful.

Regards,

Mister Z,

I understand your dissatisfaction but let me clarify things on certain points.

Here is the file again, everything is explained on the cover letter, you had to read it when you received the advertising insertion proposal !!!

My client is not a dishonest company, on the internet we read everything and the truth is not what you might think my client is the victim of unfair competition and defamation.

Take this very simple example:

If one of your competitors puts it on the Internet you are an unreliable company! Should I believe it?

The Internet is not an authority to define what a fraudulent company is, and the Internet or another company does not have to tell you not to pay your bills.
Because in this specific case, this is akin to incitement to an offense, punishable as an offense.

This contract was sent by post, Mr. Y or read it to you, signed with the stamp of the company and then returned in a pre-franked envelope for commercial purposes.

Mr. Z, no one forced Mr. M. Y to do this, I'm sorry to tell you that, but the fault lies with him.
My client doesn't have to be penalized for this.

Today I have taken your comments into account and with your agreement if you wish I am ready to negotiate this claim with my Director of Cabinet in order to limit the costs for the 2 parties.

If you accept, I will have you establish a payment / contract termination agreement in order to close this file by mutual agreement.

I am waiting for your answer.

Regards,

Hello,
So I am not Mister X but Madam.

Regarding the cover letter, I did not receive it because if I had received it, I would have read it and things would have been clear to me.

I received the form alone which, as I said before, is extremely contentious in its terms.

I have not been to the reputation of your client on the Internet, I have not needed it. Their approach was enough to make up my own mind.
If your customer is defamed on the Internet it is a good start and as they say there is no smoke without fire.

Mr X is in POPOLAND and does not speak French, this case does not concern him.

I need to discuss this with my Director and I will get back to you as soon as I get a response from him.

Regards,

Mrs. Z,

After hearing from my Chief of Staff, I was able to reduce your claim.

Please find attached the payment agreement / termination of contract to return to me (as soon as possible so that I can block your file and avoid you the bailiff) signed with the stamp of your company if you wish to close this file by amicable way.

Once signed, I will send it to my client who will do the same and I will return it to you.

In the subject of the settlement put only the file number so that our accounting department can quickly identify the payment:

000000

If you refuse to settle this claim, it is your right and I respect it.

In this case I will be forced to send your file to the bailiff no later than June 25, 2018.

Address of the cabinet of bailiffs at your disposal if you wish to pay the claim directly with them!

Regards,

Sir,

I'm waiting for my Director to return. I come back with his answer early next week because I will be absent tomorrow.

cordially

Dear,

Since the amicable confrontation with our Cabinet of judicial officers failed:

I would like to inform you that our client XYZ. will sue you in JUPITER at the court of VENUS to assert its rights.

The amount claimed will be 3 years (4,000.00 EUROS + recovery costs) as written on the contract that you have read and signed.

We are required to inform you that this legal action does not require the legal consent or the presence of your company and that the case will be decided solely on the basis of the evidence provided by the claimant which gives rise to a payment mandate. by default. The judgment will be executed in accordance with international regulations to which your country is also bound, in particular the international convention on the recognition and enforcement of foreign judgments in civil and commercial matters and the international convention on choice of court agreements.

We are also required to inform you that on the basis of similar international conflicts, we can estimate your final disbursement, including late fees, court fees and legal fees, between Euro 12,000.00 and Euro 15,000.00.

Regards,

Sir,

I send you as an attached file the response letter to the email you sent to Mr X on 09/19/2018.

Regards,

CASE N°16

Sir,

letter of 08/03/2016 and 11/04/2016 and new mail of this day to XYZ.

Handrail to the French police and report to the ABCD of CORRUPTLAND.
Internet link.

No computer file is transferred to XYZr.

I send your client one last letter and I copy the letters to you.
We have a complaint for catalog scam.

Greetings
M Z

Hello Mrs. Z,

But what scam are you talking about?

Do you associate my first name Mohamed with a scam?

On this order form, I see your signature, the stamp of your company, my client XYZ has honored the advertising service you have ordered, it is quite normal for my client to claim its due.

Your signature and the company stamp legally bind you.

You have to pay these bills!

Regards,

Hello,

I don't equate your name with XYZ. I'll let you see with your mail to process.

I will now ignore your emails because it is not an order but an abuse

It's known to the CORRUPTLAND police

The company is prohibited from publishing our products in this catalog

Good continuation
M Z

Mrs. Z,

You can ignore my emails but it will not clear the claim.

If we do not find an amicable solution your file will be transmitted to the office of bailiffs to recover this claim with the consequences that this implies.

Read the contract well, it is tacit renewal and the important thing is to terminate this contract with my client and for that I can make you a payment agreement / contract termination.

The commercial being dissociated from the criminal, the invoice must be paid.

Do I have to negotiate this claim for you?

Regards,

Hello Mrs. Z,

If you choose to ignore my emails, I will consider this an act of racism.

And I will send your file at the end of the day to our legal department.

Regards,

Madame Merle,

My colleague X sent you by email on March 13, 2018 a file concerning an unpaid invoice.

No positive reaction from you.

I would like to inform you that your file will be transmitted from Monday, March 26, 2018 to our office of bailiffs to recover this claim with the consequences that this entails (Order to pay, attachment to bank account, entry in the debtors register).

The amount claimed by the bailiff will be 2,518.15 EUROS (+ costs).

Being the mediator between you and my client for this file, I remain at your disposal.

Regards,

Sir,

You will not receive any payment from my client, the company XYZ.
At your insistence, I inform you that I will file, at the request of my client, a complaint for fraud with the Prosecutor of the Court of Appeal of VENUS with constitution of civil party.

Greetings.

XX
Associate lawyer

My Dear XX,

But what scam are you talking about?

Madame Z signed an order for an advertising service, the company XYZ honored the order and Madame Z refuses to pay for this service.

You can file a complaint, this will not erase the claim since the criminal is dissociated from the commercial.

Mrs Z has moral obligations towards the company XYZ.

This invoice must be paid.

And if you encourage Madame Z not to pay this invoice:

- You make incitement to crime ...... punishable as a crime.

The file will go to the bailiff at the end of March.

We have a few days to settle this dispute amicably.

Greetings.

Sir,

First of all I am a lawyer and I am not your Dear XX.

Second, I have nothing else to add to my previous email.

Go to the Tribunal.

Greetings.

Hello XX,

I know that you are a lawyer but above all, you are like me a human being.

If you want me to call you Master in order to flatter your oversized ego, please be kind to call me Monsignor so that my hyper-dimensioned ego is as flattered as that we will be at the same social rank (You the Notable of Province and I the Aristocrat International).

After this little clarification between Gentlemen, let's come back to this file which is starting to make you earn money thanks to my intervention!

By reading your answer and making the decision that your customer will not pay this invoice whose order form has been signed and stamped with the stamp of the company and our future appointment at the court of JUPITER, I would like to give you some information :

In my 1st email, I sent you my client's Proxy giving us full powers to collect this claim.

This means that we will proceed to a European order for payment because the order form is fully recognized by the laws of international trade in the sense that this order form has been signed and stamped by Madame Z director of XYZ and this form of order was received by my client XYZ confirming this contractual commitment on both sides.

Our client XYZ has honored his commitments but not your client XYZ.

I understand that you are working the best you can for your client, but your decision to go to court will incur additional costs for the company XYZ, unpaid invoices, your fees, accumulation of various taxes, increase in interest for payments in delay as well as your own expenses my Dear XX.

We, like you, work in the interest of our client, and would like to find together with you, if possible, the best solution to close this file amicably for the 2 parties.

Greetings,

CASE N°17

gentlemen,

We formally contest your request for payment of this invoice.

We have never signed this order.

The document that you communicate to us is obviously a forgery and its use is questionable.

If you persist in your unfounded request we will file a complaint with the public prosecutor so that the author (s) of this false document is prosecuted and sentenced.

Cordially.

Hello Mister X,

I thank you for your responsiveness.

The service provided has been visible here on this link since 2016:

Internet link.

For the record, this order form was read and signed with the stamp of the company, then this order form was sent in a pre-franked envelope for commercial purposes.

The signature as well as the stamp of the company binds you legally, the invoices must be paid.

What fake are you talking about?

Are you associating my First Name Z with fraud ???

I can in my turn, send this file (including your letter) to various organizations that you have in CORRUPTLAND which fight against racism.

You can file a complaint, this will not erase the claim since the salesperson is dissociated from the criminal.

Be kind to do a survey within your company to find out who signed this purchase order!

And legally, it does not matter who signed this order because the company is responsible for its employees.

We have until the end of March to close this file amicably and find a suitable solution for both parties (you and my client).

Awaiting your response for a possible proposal from you.

Regards,

gentlemen,
I inform you that we have filed a complaint with the Public Prosecutor at the Tribunal de Grande Instance of PLUTON for forgery and use of forgery and attempted fraud, crimes covered by articles 441.1 and 313.1 of the Penal Code.
Regards,

Dear,

My colleague Z sent you by email on March 12, 2018 a file concerning an unpaid invoice.

No positive reaction from you.

I would like to inform you that your file will be sent from Friday, March 30, 2018 to our office of bailiffs to recover this claim with the consequences that this entails (order to pay, attachment to bank account, entry in the debtors register).

The amount claimed by the bailiff will be 3,000.00 EUROS (+ costs).

Being the mediator between you and my client for this file, I remain at your disposal.

Regards,

Mister X,

I have not received any news from you for this unpaid invoice (File sent by email on March 12, 2018).

You have read my emails and you persist in your silence, this attitude shows that you are guilty and without valid arguments on this matter.

At the request of my client, I ask you one last time to settle this claim!

I am the mediator between you and my client.

If we do not find an amicable solution this week, your file will be sent to the office of bailiffs early next week.
Maybe you prefer to settle these invoices directly to the bailiff ???

Failure to pay this amount within the stipulated time will immediately result in necessary legal action against your business for the original amount plus interest, collection costs, court fees, attorney fees and expenses. In accordance with the terms of the contract, the competent court is the Court of Justice of JUPITER, the applicable law is that of VENUS.

We are required to inform you that this legal action does not require the legal consent or the presence of your company and that the case will be decided solely on the basis of the evidence provided by the claimant which gives rise to a payment mandate. by default. The judgment will be executed in accordance with international regulations to which your country is also bound, in particular the international convention on the recognition and enforcement of foreign judgments in civil and commercial matters and the international convention on choice of court agreements.

We are also required to inform you that on the basis of similar international conflicts, we can estimate your final disbursement, including late fees, court fees and legal fees, between Euro 12,000.00 and Euro 15,000.00.

Regards,

Sir,
You will find attached my answer of March 29th.

Mister X,

Your answer of March 29 is surprisingly empty, there is nothing in this attached file.

It doesn't matter because the invoices have to be paid.

It's the last day to pay these bills.

By refusing, I am sending your file to the bailiff to recover this claim from Monday 04 June 2018.

Regards,

CASE N°18

Dear,

I have not received any news from you for this unpaid invoice (File sent by email on April 10, 2018).

You have read my emails and you persist in your silence, this attitude shows that you are guilty and without valid arguments on this matter.

You have abused the trust of my client by not respecting the contract that you have read and signed.

At the request of my client, I ask you one last time to settle this claim!

I am the mediator between you and my client.

If we do not find an amicable solution this week, your file will be sent to the office of bailiffs early next week.

Maybe you prefer to settle these invoices directly to the bailiff ???

Failure to pay this amount within the stipulated time will immediately result in necessary legal action against your business for the original amount plus interest, collection costs, court fees, attorney fees and expenses. In accordance with the terms of the contract, the competent court is the Court of Justice of JUPITER, the applicable law is that of MARS.

We are required to inform you that this legal action does not require the legal consent or the presence of your company and that the case will be decided solely on the basis of the evidence provided by the claimant which gives rise to a payment mandate. by default. The judgment will be executed in accordance with international regulations to which your country is also bound, in particular the international convention on the recognition and enforcement of foreign judgments in civil and commercial matters and the international convention on choice of court agreements.

We are also required to inform you that on the basis of similar international conflicts, we can estimate your final disbursement, including late fees, court fees and legal fees, between Euro 12,000.00 and Euro 15,000.00.

Regards,

Madame, I piss you on the line. (Video).

Dear Mr. X,

Thank you for this moment of relaxation.

You are lucky to be able to relax this way while working.

Mr. X you must also PAY YOUR INVOICES before you can have fun.

Since 2016 my client has been waiting for his due.

You are a business owner, you have contractual obligations to my client with the contract that you have read and signed.

Behave like a responsible person and not like an immature child by sending a video as a response.

Regards,

CASE N°19

Hello sir,

You can inform your client that we will not pay these amounts as mentioned several times. We had denounced this contract several times.
As this is a scam, you will understand that if you insist, we will be obliged to approach the ABCD.

Regards,

Hello Mister Z,

But what scam are you talking about?

Do you associate my first name Y with a scam?

Have you sent a registered letter denouncing this contract?

You can contact any organization you want, it will not clear the invoice.

On this purchase order, I see the signature of the Director, the stamp of the company, my client XYZ honored the advertising service that you ordered, it is quite normal that my client claims its due.

Your signature and the company stamp legally bind you.

You have to pay these bills!

Regards,

Mister Z,

Hereby,

Having had no positive reaction from you.

I inform you and confirm that your file including the exchange of emails for unpaid invoices will be transmitted from Wednesday May 16, 2018 to the office of bailiffs to recover this claim with the consequences that this implies.

Greetings,

CASE N°20

Mr.
It is a huge international scam
My lawyer Maître Z has already replied to this company
If this company continues to bother us, we will sue it
A word to the wise
cordially
Mr x

Dear Sir,

Thank you for your answer.

But what scam are you talking about?

Mr. X, you should have read this entire purchase order before signing it and sending it back in a postage-paid envelope for commercial purposes.
The fault lies with you, my client is not responsible for your negligence.

You cannot escape your moral obligations as a business owner.

Your signature and the stamp of your company legally bind you.

We have this week to close this file amicably and find a suitable solution for both parties (you and my client).

Awaiting your response for a possible proposal from you.

Regards,

Mr.
The scams are well known we are well informed
Your client at the contact details of my lawyer
He can come back to him to summon me to court
I will forward your correspondence to my lawyer
cordially
Mr x

Sir,

The contract is MARTIAN, that risked costing you a fortune.

Does your lawyer have a license to practice on MARS?

If no one represents you in the JUPITER court, you will be condemned by default.

And if we do not find an amicable solution this week, your file will be sent to the office of bailiffs to collect this claim.

Regards,

Mr.
Do what you have to do, the court of VENUS and the repression of fraud will take over the case now, any act or letter will be sent to my master lawyer Z Lawyer at the Court
cordially
Mr x

Sir,

The commercial being dissociated from the criminal, this will not erase the claim.

My work is certainly hated but honest.

I will keep your file until the end of this week.

Regards,

Mr you work yourself with a dishonest company which makes a criminal association for you and your company and this makes you an accomplice before the law
Then it's up to you to take responsibility
It's just a warning

Sir,

You have a lot of imagination and have been in this profession for many years, threats and other sterile warnings no longer have any effect.

Currently you are not assuming your responsibilities, no one has forced you to fill out this order form and even less to return this order form in a prepaid envelope for commercial purposes.

I am in contact with you to help you on this file, for me it is very easy to find a possibility of reduction of the receivable, for that I can go to see my Director of cabinet but you refuse my help.

The intervention of your lawyer will not change anything.

You have 3 days to pay this invoice!

Regards,

You are a band of charlot
So go find another pigeon
But maybe you are a pigeon yourself
In your case to react

Dear Sir,

You start with the insults:

- you are lacking in arguments.
- You're losing your temper.

These links that you sent me have no legal power.

But what is certain is that you refuse to pay these bills because other companies on the internet recommend that you do not pay them.

This is called incitement to an offense punishable as an offense.

These companies engage in unfair competition.

You have 2 days to settle these invoices.

Regards,

CASE N°21

Mister X,

After hearing from my Director of Cabinet, I was able to reduce this debt to you.

Enclosed is the payment agreement / contract termination to be returned to me signed as soon as possible so that I can block your file to prevent you from being served by a bailiff.

The RIB is also attached.

For the purpose of the payment, put only your file number so that our accounts can quickly identify your payment:

000000

If you refuse, it is your right and I respect it, in this case I will be forced to transmit your file to our office of bailiffs to recover this claim with the consequences that this implies, costs will be added by the bailiff.

Awaiting your response.

Regards,

Hello,

I acknowledge receipt of your proposal.
In order to be able to answer it, you can send me items that can help us assess the service billed.
Diffusion of the directory, referencing of the site, Feeds and datas of the visits on the page in question ...

Thank you
Good captain

Mister X,

Your advertisement has been active since 2016 on the link I gave you in my previous email.

Concerning the referencing of the site, feeds and datas of the visits, I do debt collection, this is not my responsibility.

But by typing the name of your company on G .... (not to mention it!) You appear on the 1st page, which I think is very good!

Internet link.

Regards,
Hello Mister Y,

Before settlement, we need a copy of the agreement / termination dated, signed and stamped with the name of the signatory.

Thank you in advance.
Best regards,

Hello Mrs. Z,

I'm sending the payment agreement to my client and I'm coming back to you probably tomorrow morning.

Regards,

Mrs. Z,

Attached is the payment agreement / contract termination signed by my client to return me signed as soon as possible so that I can block your file to avoid you being served by a bailiff.

The RIB is also attached.

For the purpose of the payment, put only your file number so that our accounts can quickly identify your payment:

000000

Regards,

Hello Mister Y,

After careful consideration, we have decided not to pay the sum of € 5,000.00 for the reasons set out below.

The form is clearly intended to be confused with one of the many forms necessary for participation in the ABCD Fair. Thus, we were misled when we received this letter in 2015.

We were never contacted by the company in question before your telephone reminder in early 2018.
We doubt the existence of both society and service. Indeed, the headers, recipients of banking entities covering etc. show all the names of different entities and domiciled in different countries each time.

The information available on the internet, about your client clearly shows a FRAUD.
Examples
Internet link.
Internet link.

Internet link.
Internet link.

The service offered for sale by your customer is not clearly identifiable. We have interviewed many of our clients, none of whom know the directory in question.

Finally, XYZ management seems to know your client's practices and clearly identify them as fraudulent with its members.

So we were abused.

Mister X,

I read your mail carefully.

You are in the process of shirking and looking for all the pretexts in order to not pay this bill.

No fraud, no judgment rendered by a court.

The show organizer defames and acts of unfair competition.

I note that you have never been contacted by my client before my email.
No luck for you because we have on file for 2016 email exchanges with my client by yourself on 03/31/2016, 04/04/2016 and 08/04/2016.

You doubt the existence of the company and the service rendered!

Here is the link again, an active service since 2016:

Internet link.

Before so much bad faith on your part, I inform you that your file will be sent to the bailiff today at 5:00 p.m. if the payment is not made and if the payment agreement is not returned to me signed by your go.

Regards,

Hello Mrs. Z,

I remind you that this is the last day to return the signed payment agreement and proof of transfer to me.

Without these 2 documents, I will be forced to transmit this file today at 5:00 p.m. to the bailiff to recover this claim.
Regards,

CASE N°22

Sir,

you work for a scam?

Internet link.

We are not concerned !! We never filled anything !!

Mrs. Y,

Are you associating my First Name Z with a scam ???

I can in my turn, send this file (including your letter) to various organizations that you have in CORRUPTLAND which fight against racism.

Does this suit you?

Mrs. Y, you should have read this entire purchase order before signing it and sending it back in a prepaid envelope for commercial purposes.
The fault lies with you, my client is not responsible for your negligence.

You cannot escape your moral obligations as a business owner.

We have this week to close this file amicably and find a suitable solution for both parties (you and my client).

Awaiting your response for a possible proposal from you.

Regards,

Mrs. Y,

What is your link?

Take responsibility.

Regards,

Mrs. Y,

ASSUME WHAT YOU SIGNED !!!

AND ESPECIALLY READ A DOCUMENT IN FULL BEFORE SIGNING AND RETURNING IT.

You must understand that you are solely responsible for this situation, no one has forced you to fill out this order form and then return it in a pre-paid envelope for commercial purposes.

Today you are in conflict with yourself through your own neglect.

If you prefer to pay directly to the bailiff I give you his contact details as well as a payment agreement / contract termination.

CASE N°23

Hello Mister X,

I remind you that this is the last day to return the signed payment agreement and proof of transfer to me.

Without these 2 documents, I will be forced to transmit this file today at 5:00 p.m. to the bailiff to recover this claim.

Regards,

Hello Gentlemen,

Following the extraordinary general meeting that we convened last week to discuss your file, our partners and I have decided to make you a proposal. To respect the laws of our country as well as possible, this proposal was sent to you by registered mail with acknowledgment of receipt and posted yesterday Thursday 03 May 2018. You should receive this proposal at the latest Monday. I await your return once you have read the said proposal.

Regards,

Mister X,

On April 18, 2014, my colleague Z sent you the complete file for this unpaid invoice.

No positive reaction from you.

I would like to inform you that your file will be transmitted from Monday, April 30, 2018 to our office of bailiffs to recover this claim with the consequences that this entails (Order to pay, attachment to bank account, entry in the debtors register).

The amount claimed by the bailiff will be 5,000, 00 EUROS (+ costs).

Finally, please inform your Direction as soon as possible for this file, no additional delay will be accepted.

Being the mediator between you and my client for this file, I remain at your disposal for a possible proposal from you.

Regards,

Hello,

Our lawyers are on the file. Apparently there would be a forgery and use of forgeries and identity theft on the part of your customer on the order form, we will not fail to make you a return.

In addition, having the chance to work in close collaboration with the judicial police services within the framework of our activity, the latter advised us to bring the case before the judge, something that we will not fail to do once our lawyers will have drafted the request.

Dear Mr. X,

I thank you for your responsiveness.

I would like to remind you that you received this order form by direct mail, then you read, completed and signed it with the stamp of your company.
Then you put it in a pre-paid postage envelope for mailing, then mailed it.

No one forced you to do this.

Sorry to tell you that but the fault is yours, my client is not responsible for your negligence.

My client has honored his advertising service since 2016, still active here:

Internet link.

This technique of not paying your bills doesn't work with me, neither do your attempts to intimidate the police.

I do a hated but honest job.

In addition for your information, on 07/07/2016 you sent my client an email regarding your dissatisfaction.

So Mr. X, do you still want to continue in bad faith?

Or we can find an amicable solution to close this file quickly and easily.

I remain at your disposal if you have a proposal for me.

Keep in mind that this is a tacit renewal contract, a contract termination will be established at your request.

Otherwise, your file will be sent to the bailiff at the end of this week.

Regards,

Mister X,

Enclosed is the payment agreement / contract termination to be returned to me signed as soon as possible so that I can block your file to prevent you from being served by a bailiff.

The RIB is also attached.

For the purpose of the payment, put only your file number so that our accounts can quickly identify your payment:

- 000000
-
If you refuse, it is your right and I respect it, in this case I will be forced to transmit your file to our office of bailiffs to recover this claim with the consequences that this implies, costs will be added by the bailiff.

Awaiting your response.

Regards,

Hello,

We must meet with our partners this weekend to act on a decision. Following this meeting, I will come back to you to notify you of the offer we will make to you to put an end to this disagreement,

Regards,

Hello Mister X,

I remind you that this is the last day to return the signed payment agreement and proof of transfer to me.

Without these 2 documents, I will be forced to transmit this file today at 5:00 p.m. to the bailiff to recover this claim.

Regards,

Hello Gentlemen,

Following the extraordinary general meeting that we convened last week to discuss your file, our partners and I have decided to make you a proposal. To respect the laws of our country as well as possible, this proposal was sent to you by registered mail with acknowledgment of receipt and posted yesterday Thursday 03 May 2018. You should receive this proposal at the latest Monday. I await your return once you have read the said proposal.

Regards,

Mister X,

Thank you for your answer.

Having experience in debt collection, I know that your "proposal" will likely be a letter from a lawyer or something similar.

Since you refuse to settle this invoice, I must send your file today at 5:00 p.m. to the bailiff.

Greetings,

Ah no, I totally register as a fake! This letter is a proposal written by us and not by our lawyers, you will see for yourself

Mister X,

The payment / contract termination agreement that I sent to you is valid until today.

Send me your proposal by email, you still have time to scan your mail.

I have deadlines that I cannot break.

Greetings,

unfortunately I can not scan it since it went to the mail ... you will receive it Monday without fail

Mister X,

What do you mean ?
You didn't even keep a copy?

You take this situation as a game.

I wasted enough time on this file.

I am sending your file to the bailiff now, no need to wait until 5:00 p.m.

Greetings

Hello,

Can I send you the proposal by email or is it too late?

Mister X,

Hereby,

I inform you and confirm that your file including the exchange of emails for unpaid invoices has been sent to the office of bailiffs to recover this claim with the consequences that this implies.

Greetings

Mister X,

Since the amicable confrontation with our Cabinet of judicial officers failed:

I would like to inform you that our client XYZ. will sue you in POPOLAND in the court of VENUS to assert its rights.

The amount claimed will be 3 years (4,000.00 EUROS + recovery costs) as written on the contract that you have read and signed.

We are required to inform you that this legal action does not require the legal consent or the presence of your company and that the case will be decided solely on the basis of the evidence provided by the claimant which gives rise to a payment mandate. by default. The judgment will be executed in accordance with international regulations to which your country is also bound, in particular the international convention on the recognition and enforcement of foreign judgments in civil and commercial matters and the international convention on choice of court agreements.

We are also required to inform you that on the basis of similar international conflicts, we can estimate your final disbursement, including late fees, court fees and legal fees, between Euro 12,000.00 and Euro 15,000.00.

I keep your file until September 24, 2018.

Regards,

Hello Mister Z,

First you have canceled the amicable confrontation on your own before it takes place.

Secondly, I'm going to send you some of the elements that we have that prevent us from responding favorably to you.
Thirdly, I would ask you to communicate to me the articles of law on which you rely because you are required to inform us but you do not give us anything specific. This is not at all clear to us.

thank you in advance

The XYZ team

Hello Mister X,

Thank-you for your prompt response.

Let me remind you of these facts:

This order form with cover letter was sent by publi postage (postal mail).

This purchase order was read, then signed and returned in a pre-paid envelope for commercial purposes.

Mr. X as far as I know, no one forced you to do this, sorry to write this but the fault lies with you, my client is not responsible for this negligence.

The cover letter clearly explained the commercial offer, Mr. X you should have read this letter in its entirety as well as the order form before sending it back to my client.

And since 2016 my client has honored the requested advertising service:

Internet link.

You created this situation yourself and now you are accusing my client of all the evils on earth.

I took into account what you sent me, the FUNNYLAND company is not my client, so no relation.

As previously announced in my email, I keep your file until September 24, 2018.

I am the mediator for this file between you and my client, let's try to negotiate this claim this week.
Please understand that personally it will not change anything for me whether you pay or not.
My function within this company is to avoid you the future conviction as well as exorbitant costs.

Do you have a proposal for me?

Otherwise don't bother blocking your file until September 24, 2018.

Regards,

Hello Mister X,

Here we are on the last day.

I have not received any offers from you.

Your file will therefore be sent to my client at the end of this day.

Regards,

CASE N°24

Mrs. Z,

PAY YOUR INVOICES !!!

If you prefer to pay directly to the bailiff I give you his contact details as well as a payment agreement / contract termination.

Regards,

Leave us alone !!!!!!

Mrs. Z,

You have to understand that I do my collection work, you have bills to pay!

You have the choice, settle these invoices at our collection office or directly at the bailiff!

I will have you establish a payment / contract termination agreement at your request.

Madam Z, you have to assume what you signed, that's all!

To have "peace" as you say, you have to pay these bills because after the bailiff will put even more pressure on you.

Regards,

Dear,

I have not received any news from you for this unpaid invoice (File sent by email on April 25, 2018).

At the request of my client, I ask you one last time to settle this claim!

I am the mediator between you and my client.

If we do not find an amicable solution this week, your file will be sent to the office of bailiffs early next week.

Maybe you prefer to settle these invoices directly to the bailiff ???

Regards,

Hello

In order to accede to your request please send us your invoice because internally, we do not know what it is,
cordially

Dear Madam,

Here is the complete file again.

My client has honored his advertising service since 2016 !!!

Internet link.

Thanks for doing what's needed.

No more delays will be tolerated.

Address of our office of bailiffs at your disposal if you prefer to pay directly to its study (additional costs will be expected).

I am blocking your file until June 4, 2018.

Maybe you prefer to settle these invoices directly to the bailiff ???

Failure to pay this amount within the stipulated time will immediately result in necessary legal action against your business for the original amount plus interest, collection costs, court fees, attorney fees and expenses. In accordance with the terms of the contract, the competent court is the Court of Justice of JUPITER, the applicable law is that of VENUS.

We are required to inform you that this legal action does not require the legal consent or the presence of your company and that the case will be decided solely on the basis of the evidence provided by the claimant which gives rise to a payment mandate. by default. The judgment will be executed in accordance with international regulations to which your country is also bound, in particular the international convention on the recognition and enforcement of foreign judgments in civil and commercial matters and the international convention on choice of court agreements.

We are also required to inform you that on the basis of similar international conflicts, we can estimate your final disbursement, including late fees, court fees and legal fees, between Euro 12,000.00 and Euro 15,000.00.

Regards,

We know it's a scam so you can stop your claims
This supplier is also informed of your scams !!!!

Dear,

I have not received any news from you for this unpaid invoice (File sent by email on May 31, 2018).

You have read my emails and you persist in your silence, this attitude shows that you are guilty and without valid arguments on this matter.

At the request of my client, I ask you one last time to settle this claim!

I am the mediator between you and my client.

If we do not find an amicable solution this week, your file will be sent to the office of bailiffs early next week.

Maybe you prefer to settle these invoices directly to the bailiff ???

Regards,

I forward your email to the police station which will take care of investigating you !!!!
Go make yourself even with your threats….

Dear,

But what threats are you talking about?

I'm just informing you of the current situation.

What exactly is a complaint?
To avoid paying your bills?

If you do that, please be kind enough to send me a duplicate.

My work is certainly hated but honest.

By filing a complaint you are going to make the situation worse; a false declaration is a criminal offense.

PAY YOUR INVOICES !!!

Regards,

We have contacted this supplier being up to date with our payments and he confirms that we have never used your servicesDonc arrêter vos bêtises…..et laisser nous travailler

Dear Madame Z,

You are probably mistaken.

No nonsense on my part.

My client is XYZ and you have 2 invoices to pay.

READ ALL THE DOCUMENTS I SENT TO YOU IN MY EMAIL OF MAY 31, 2018.

PAY YOUR INVOICES OR OTHERWISE I TRANSMIT YOUR FILE TO THE OWNER TODAY AT THE END OF THE AFTERNOON.

Mrs. Z,

Behave like a responsible business owner, take responsibility for what you sign.

PAY YOUR INVOICES !!!

In the worst case, pay a minimum of 1 year (2000 euros) to get rid of this claim, otherwise I or the bailiff will continue the reminders so that this claim is settled once and for all.

If you prefer to pay directly to the bailiff I give you his contact details as well as a payment agreement / contract termination.

Regards,

Leave us alone
We know these bullshit

Mrs. Z,

PAY YOUR INVOICES !!!

If you prefer to pay directly to the bailiff I give you his contact details as well as a payment agreement / contract termination.

Regards,

Dear,

Since the amicable confrontation with our Cabinet of judicial officers failed:

I would like to inform you that our client XYZ. will sue you on VENUS in the court of JUPITER to assert its rights.

The amount claimed will be 3 years (5000, 00 EUROS + recovery costs) as written on the contract that you have signed.

We are required to inform you that this legal action does not require the legal consent or the presence of your company and that the case will be decided solely on the basis of the evidence provided by the claimant which gives rise to a payment mandate. by default. The judgment will be executed in accordance with international regulations to which your country is also bound, in particular the international convention on the recognition and enforcement of foreign judgments in civil and commercial matters and the international convention on choice of court agreements.

I remind you that this contract is tacit renewal.

As your mediator I keep your file until April 26, 2019.

Regards,

Ah here you are again
I filed a plaint against you in 2018
I know very well that it is a scam
So don't get tired of harassing me with your emails

Hello,

We are still awaiting payment of invoices.

Please do what is necessary as soon as possible.

Regards,

We know it's a scam, so don't get tired with us anymore !!!!!!

CASE N°25

HA HA HA

She is really nice
A B C D E
ha ha ha

I send your mail to MY FRIENDS of the ABCDE
poor of you
I know them personally

I think you will find takers

Mrs. Z,

I thank you for your responsiveness.

The service provided has been visible here on this link since 2016:

Internet link.

For the record, you have read and signed this order form, then this order form has been sent in a prepaid envelope for commercial purposes.

The signature commits you legally, the invoices must be paid.

Are you associating my First Name XX with a fraudulent act ???

I can in my turn, send this file (including your email) to various organizations that you have in BULLLAND which are fighting against racism.

You can file a complaint, this will not erase the claim since the salesperson is dissociated from the criminal.

We have until the end of March to close this file amicably and find a suitable solution for both parties (you and my client).

Awaiting your response for a possible proposal from you.

Regards,

HA HA HA!

YOUR CUSTOMER I KNOW IT
YOU RADOTE AND HARASS US
BE CAREFUL, YOU ARE PLAYING A DANGEROUS GAME

Mrs. Z,

I'm not drooling!

I'm not harassing you, I do my hated but honest collections job and I don't play any games.

You seem to mind that I am called XX?

You should take responsibility for what you sign, you are a business owner and you have moral obligations.

If we do not find a suitable solution for both parties (you and my client), your file will be sent to the bailiff to collect this claim.

Regards,

Mr.

ABCDE has nothing to do with PLUTON, nor PLUTON district.
I will put your contact and your emails in the hands of the authorities who will know how to pin you
that's all

Dear,

My colleague XX sent you by email on March 19, 2018 a file concerning an unpaid invoice.

No positive reaction from you.

I would like to inform you that your file will be sent from Friday, March 30, 2018 to our office of bailiffs to recover this claim with the consequences that this entails (order to pay, attachment to bank account, entry in the debtors register).

The amount claimed by the bailiff will be 6,000.00 USD (+ costs).

Being the mediator between you and my client for this file, I remain at your disposal.

Regards,

prove it to me !!!!

Sent from my i ……

Hello Madam,

I will ask Mr. XX to send you this file.

Greetings.

I want to see it !!!!!!
rest assured that your communications will be redirected to the right place… to the POLICE !!!

CASE N°26

Hello
There is no question of paying them anything
No purchase order or even any request was made to them
These people are pure crooks

Mister X,

Thank-you for your prompt response.

I understand your dissatisfaction but you should have read this order form in full before signing it with the stamp of the company.
In addition, you have returned this order form in a prepaid envelope for commercial purposes.

Sorry to tell you that but the fault is yours, my client is not responsible for your negligence.

Know that I have nothing against you, but we must close this file by mutual agreement or I will be forced to forward your file to the bailiff.

This is a tacit renewal contract, it must be terminated to avoid the accumulation of invoices.

Would you like me to issue a contract termination to you?

Regards,

I NEVER signed anything with them
They are crooks in due form

Mister X,

You or another person in your company has signed this order form.

And it does not matter who signed this order because the company is responsible for its employees.

To date my client has not been convicted, you are just defaming.

Would you like me to issue a contract termination to you?

Do you have a proposal for me?

Regards,

Your customer has used an order form from the company XYZ with whom I subscribed my presence at a trade show
I did nothing else

There can be no termination of contract since there is no contract between them and us!

Mister X,

Hereby,

Having had no positive reaction from you.

I inform you and confirm that your file including the exchange of emails for unpaid invoices will be transmitted from Tuesday 15 May 2018 to the office of bailiffs to recover this claim with the consequences that this implies.

Greetings

Mister X,

I have not received any news from you for this unpaid invoice (File sent by email on April 25, 2018).

You have read my emails and you persist in your silence, this attitude shows that you are guilty and without valid arguments on this matter.

At the request of my client, I ask you one last time to settle this claim!

I am the mediator between you and my client.

If we do not find an amicable solution this week, your file will be sent to the office of bailiffs early next week.

Maybe you prefer to settle these invoices directly to the bailiff ???

Failure to pay this amount within the stipulated time will immediately result in necessary legal action against your business for the original amount plus interest, collection costs, court fees, attorney fees and expenses. In accordance with the terms of the contract, the competent court is the Court of Justice of JUPITER, the applicable law is that of VENUS.

We are required to inform you that this legal action does not require the legal consent or the presence of your company and that the case will be decided solely on the basis of the evidence provided by the claimant which gives rise to a payment mandate. by default. The judgment will be executed in accordance with international regulations to which your country is also bound, in particular the international convention on the recognition and enforcement of foreign judgments in civil and commercial matters and the international convention on choice of court agreements.

We are also required to inform you that on the basis of similar international conflicts, we can estimate your final disbursement, including late fees, court fees and legal fees, between Euro 12,000.00 and Euro 15,000.00.

Regards,

Mister X,

You have abused the trust of my client by not respecting the contract that you have read and signed.

Behave like a responsible business owner.

PAY YOUR INVOICES !!!

In the worst case, pay a minimum of 1 year (2000 euros) to get rid of this claim, otherwise I or the bailiff will continue the reminders so that this claim is settled once and for all.

Regards,

CASE N°27

Hello,
As informed in 2016 during the first false invoice, this does not concern us at all.
There has been identity theft.
I kindly ask you to regularize the situation as soon as possible.
Cordially.

Hello,

I thank you for your responsiveness.

I would like to remind you that you received this order form by direct mail, then you read, completed and signed it with the stamp of your company.
Then you put it in a pre-paid postage envelope for mailing, then mailed it.

No one forced you to do this.

Sorry to tell you that but the fault is yours, my client is not responsible for your negligence.

My client has honored his advertising service since 2016, still active here:

Internet link.

I do a hated but honest job.
Are you associating my first name XX with something illegal?

I confirm that you have actually sent an email to my client on 03/21/2016 by writing that you have completed this order form.

So no identity theft and even less false invoices.

Do you still want to continue in bad faith?

Or we can find an amicable solution to close this file quickly and easily.

I remain at your disposal if you have a proposal for me.

Keep in mind that this is a tacit renewal contract, a contract termination will be established at your request.

Otherwise, your file will be sent to the bailiff at the end of this week.

Address of our office of bailiffs available at your request.

Regards,
Sir,
The document which was sent to the company XYZ spanked following the fair in which we had participated, was diverted thereafter and that is why I speak of false invoice.

Let me tell you, which I find inappropriate, to mention any judgment on my part towards your first name, also being of immigrant origin.
Our legal department had researched this so-called company and advised us to stop communicating.
You can contact me by phone on 00 00 00 00 00.
cordially

Mrs,

Hereby,

Having had no positive reaction from you.

I inform you and confirm that your file including the exchange of emails for unpaid invoices will be transmitted from Tuesday 15 May 2018 to the office of bailiffs to recover this claim with the consequences that this implies.

Greetings

CASE N°28

Dear Sir,

As previously indicated in 2016 to this service provider, based on JUPITER and whose payment must take place for a bank on VENUS, we firmly dispute these 2 invoices for which we do not benefit from any form of service.
We also questioned the order form, the signature of which did not comply with a member of the XYZ staff.
Besides, no XYZ contact appears on the order form.

I would be grateful if you would take into consideration these elements of dispute and kindly close this file.

Thanking you in advance,

cordially
Mr. X

Mister X,

Thank-you for your prompt response.

I understand your dissatisfaction.

Legally, it does not matter who signed this order form because you are responsible for your employees.

Your organization within your company cannot question the invoices to be paid as well as the order form, my client has honored his advertising service which has been active since 2016:

Internet link.

We work with the whole world and our Director of Cabinet has chosen a bank on VENUS (European Union) because the bank charges are the lowest.

I cannot close this file, we must find an amicable solution suitable for both parties, I remain open to any proposals from you.

Being the mediator between you and my client for this file, I remain at your disposal.

Greetings,

Mister Z,

I do not share your legal analysis, as indicated below the signature on the order form does not belong to a person of the XYZ, we deduce that this is similar to a forgery.
In addition, we have no contact with suppliers based on JUPITER.

However, as part of a proof, could you send us a copy of the email received by the service provider justifying the order.

Thanking you in advance,

cordially
Mr. X

Mister X,

In my 1st email, you have the file with all the elements.

It cannot be a forgery, this order form you received it by direct mail, then signed (you or another person of your company) with the stamp of the company, returned in a pre-franked envelope for purpose commercial.

The stamp of your company binds you legally.

Perhaps you prefer to settle directly with the bailiff?

Regards,

Dear Mr. Z,

The attached documents are incomplete and do not comply with our internal purchasing process.
At the risk of repeating it, the order form for your previous email is not referenced in our database and the signature does not correspond to a member of the XYZ staff.

We are unable to pay the invoices in good condition and we would like to have a copy of our validation email or any other supporting documents.

Pending a return to our requests,

cordially
Mr. X

Mister X,

Here again is the order form, I have highlighted in yellow the terms of the contract, the signature as well as the stamp of the company act of validation of this contract.

I am not responsible and even less my client if this purchase order is not referenced in your database, your work organization should not penalize my client.

Regards,

Mister X,

Hereby,

Having had no positive reaction from you concerning these 2 unpaid invoices since 2016.

I inform you and confirm that your file for unpaid invoices will be transmitted from Friday, May 18, 2018 to the office of bailiffs to recover this claim with the consequences that this implies.

Greetings,

Mister X,

I have not received any news from you for this unpaid invoice (File sent by email on April 25, 2018).

You have read my emails and you persist in your silence, this attitude shows that you are guilty and without valid arguments on this matter.

At the request of my client, I ask you one last time to settle this claim!

I am the mediator between you and my client.

If we do not find an amicable solution this week, your file will be sent to the office of bailiffs early next week.

Maybe you prefer to settle these invoices directly to the bailiff ???

Failure to pay this amount within the stipulated time will immediately result in necessary legal action against your business for the original amount plus interest, collection costs, court fees, attorney fees and expenses. In accordance with the terms of the contract, the competent court is the Court of Justice of JUPITER, the applicable law is that of VENUS.

We are required to inform you that this legal action does not require the legal consent or the presence of your company and that the case will be decided solely on the basis of the evidence provided by the claimant which gives rise to a payment mandate. by default. The judgment will be executed in accordance with international regulations to which your country is also bound, in particular the international convention on the recognition and enforcement of foreign judgments in civil and commercial matters and the international convention on choice of court agreements.

We are also required to inform you that on the basis of similar international conflicts, we can estimate your final disbursement, including late fees, court fees and legal fees, between Euro 12,000.00 and Euro 15,000.00.

Regards,

Mister X,

You have abused the trust of my client by not respecting the contract that you have read and signed.

Behave like a responsible business owner.

PAY YOUR INVOICES !!!

cordially

CASE N°29

Mister X,

I have not received any news from you for this unpaid invoice (File sent by email on May 30, 2018).

You have read my emails and you persist in your silence, this attitude shows that you are guilty and without valid arguments on this matter.

You have abused the trust of my client by not respecting the contract that you have read and signed.

At the request of my client, I ask you one last time to settle this claim!

I am the mediator between you and my client.

If we do not find an amicable solution this week, your file will be sent to the office of bailiffs early next week.

Maybe you prefer to settle these invoices directly to the bailiff ???

Failure to pay this amount within the stipulated time will immediately result in necessary legal action against your business for the original amount plus interest, collection costs, court fees, attorney fees and expenses. In accordance with the terms of the contract, the competent court is the Court of Justice of JUPITER, the applicable law is that of MARS.

We are required to inform you that this legal action does not require the legal consent or the presence of your company and that the case will be decided solely on the basis of the evidence provided by the claimant which gives rise to a payment mandate. by default. The judgment will be executed in accordance with international regulations to which your country is also bound, in particular the international convention on the recognition and enforcement of foreign judgments in civil and commercial matters and the international convention on choice of court agreements.

We are also required to inform you that on the basis of similar international conflicts, we can estimate your final disbursement, including late fees, court fees and legal fees, between Euro 12,000.00 and Euro 15,000.00.

Regards,

JUPITER's jurisdiction, really?

Mister X,

I will ask you a little seriously for this file.

If you refuse to close this file by mutual agreement, please inform me and I transfer this file today to the bailiff to collect this claim.

Does that suit you?

Regards,

No thanks

Dear,

These invoices must be paid.

If you refuse to settle these invoices by mutual agreement then in this case I will send your file at the end of this week to the bailiff in order to recover this claim.

Charges will be added by the bailiff.

Regards,

Okay

Dear,

It's heard !

So I will send your file Friday June 15, 2018 at 10:00 am to the bailiff to collect this claim entailing additional costs.

I note that you prefer to settle this claim directly with the bailiff.

I understand you, it is much easier for you, you are in CORRUPTLAND and we are abroad.

Regards,

Hello Mister X,

I have not received any news from you for this unpaid invoice (File sent by email on April 23, 2018).

At the request of my client, I ask you one last time to settle this claim!

I am the mediator between you and my client.

If we do not find an amicable solution this week, your file will be sent to the office of bailiffs early next week.

Maybe you prefer to settle these invoices directly to the bailiff ???

Regards,

Hello Mister Z,

Could you enlighten me on the subject? I am not informed of any claim to be settled.

Who is your client?

Yours

CASE N°30

Sir,

I find your conclusion "No further delay will be tolerated" interesting.
What I no longer tolerate for my part are the methods used by your customers.
We will therefore analyze the follow-up to your message.
cordially

Hello Mister X,

Thank-you for your prompt response.

I understand your dissatisfaction but this purchase order, you received it by direct mail (postal mail) then read, filled and signed.
Then you sent this order form in a pre-paid envelope for commercial purposes.

No one forced you to do this.

You should have read this entire contract, it is your fault, my client is not responsible for your negligence.

Enclosed is the payment agreement / contract termination to be returned to me signed as soon as possible so that I can block your file to prevent you from being served by a bailiff.

The RIB is also attached.

For the purpose of the payment, put only your file number so that our accounts can quickly identify your payment:

   -000000

If you refuse, it is your right and I respect it, in this case I will be forced to transmit your file to our office of bailiffs to recover this claim with the consequences that this implies, costs will be added by the bailiff.

Regards,

Hello sir,

Thank you for your detailed argument, indeed nobody forced me, fortunately besides.
However the principle of sale is close to the scam, which explains my position.
The formatting of the "order form" suggests that it is a compulsory formality to participate in the fair. It is this commercial technique that I do not tolerate.
Yours

Dear,

Hereby,

Having had no positive reaction from you concerning these 2 unpaid invoices since 2016.

I inform you and confirm that your file for unpaid invoices will be transmitted from Friday, May 18, 2018 to the office of bailiffs to recover this claim with the consequences that this implies.

Greetings,

Hello sir,

I just came back from a long trip to FUNNYLAND which explains my lack of reaction.
I inform you that I do not feel at all "guilty" as you suggest, it is the approach of your client that is questioning.
I will therefore contact my legal counsel to deal with this matter.
Yours

Mister X,

You have abused the trust of my client by not respecting the contract that you have read and signed.

Behave like a responsible business owner.

PAY YOUR INVOICES !!!

In the worst case, pay a minimum of 1 year (2000 euros) to get rid of this claim, otherwise I or the bailiff will continue the reminders so that this claim is settled once and for all.

cordially

CASE N°31

Mrs. Z,

After hearing from my Chief of Staff, I was able to reduce your claim.

Please find attached the payment agreement / termination of contract to return to me (as soon as possible so that I can block your file and avoid you the bailiff) signed with the stamp of your company if you wish to close this file by amicable way.

Once signed, I will send it to my client who will do the same and I will return it to you.

In the subject of the settlement put only the file number so that our accounting department can quickly identify the payment:

000000

If you refuse to settle this claim, it is your right and I respect it.

In this case I will be forced to transmit your file to the bailiff no later than July 25, 2018 to recover this claim with the consequences that this implies.

Regards,

Sir,
I answer you the same as on the phone. The company for which you are mandated, operates like a real scammer business. It is out of the question to settle this excessive amount. Even the corporate structure is opaque.
I will not pay this amount, you can mandate the bailiff now if you wish. But it is clear that in this case, this case will not stop there.
Regards,

Mrs. Z,

I am in contact with you to close this file by mutual agreement, so I ask you a little serious and avoid talking about scammers!

You libel for free, which is unprofessional on your part.

I would like to remind you of these important facts:

This order form with cover letter was sent by publi postage (postal mail).

This purchase order was read, then signed and returned in a pre-paid envelope for commercial purposes.

Madam Z as far as I know, no one forced Ms. Y to do this, sorry to write this but the fault lies with her, my client is not responsible for this negligence.

And since 2016 my client has honored the requested advertising service:

Internet link

An order form must be read in full.

Now do what you want, I'm just an employee who does his job and who wants to avoid you the bailiff.

By refusing this payment agreement, the contract will not be terminated and the 3rd invoice will follow in a few weeks.

Regards,

Let me disagree with your statements.
Now do what you want, I will do what I want.

CASE N°32

Mister X,
PAY YOUR INVOICES !!!
If you prefer to pay directly to the bailiff I give you his contact details as well as a payment agreement / contract termination.
Regards,

ATTENTION: You are in the European watch list for fraud. waist your time elsewhere.

Mister X,

Which kind fraud?

Do you associate my origins name to a fraud?

Be careful I could pursuit you to the court for that.

So you must pay your invoices or may be do you prefer pay directly to bailiff ???

Regards.

Dear Y,

for your information:
Definitions of fraud

noun
wrongful or criminal deception intended to result in financial or personal gain.

Tell me how does it make you feel to work for a company that cheats people, a band of "scams", hidden in phantoms companies. I do wonder how many people falls into your dishonest tricks to pay your salary.
get the facts straight, I can prove that I didn't sign any contract with the company that you make me believe you are representing and didn't even participate to the show that they invent the service was for.
You have no idea who you are talking to, where I am ... and you want to take me to court. Dream off my dear Mr. FRAUD
Fun talking to you.
Mister X,

As you are a liar and don't have any respect about my job and my origins, I will send your file to the bailiff today.

The bailiff will add the fees.

Regards.

Ok, momo, what else do you want?

Mister X,

Please respect my name.

I just need to know if you want directly your invoices to bailiff?

Regards.

Dear Sir

It seems to me that you don't really realize that your client is a fraudulent business. How do you want me to pay for something I didn't ask for and, in fact, I didn't even participate in the exhibit they claim to have done. They ask me to pay for something that I participated in 2015 and not in 2016.

Indeed, we have received an email from the organizers of the exhibition on the scam of the fraudulent company which you belong to or which you represent.

So if you haven't realized it yet, I am having fun replying to your email.

You will get nothing from me and this is the last email, from now on, you are going to spam

Please get correct and honest work.

Cheers

CASE N°33

Sir,

You are an accomplice of an international scam company.
If you continue to annoy us, we will seize the services of the public prosecutor and the tax authorities against you and this company and inform the respective embassies of JUPITER, VENUS and PLUTON.

In addition, in your email, you will want to indicate the legal notices of your organization as well as the names and quality of the people who act.

We already have a file on the company "XYZ".

There is no question of paying any amount of money.

Accounting department.

Dear,

But what scam are you talking about?

Do you have an official link where my client was sentenced for X reasons?

I do a hated but honest job.

Do you want to file a complaint?

What is the purpose of not paying the bills?

The commercial being dissociated from the criminal, this will not erase the invoices and making a false declaration will backfire on you when the bailiff will have the file if you refuse to settle this claim out of court.

My client is a victim of defamation and unfair competition.

If I read slanderous articles about your company on the internet, should I believe them?

Let me remind you of these facts:

This order form with cover letter was sent by publi postage (postal mail).

This purchase order was read, then signed with the stamp of the company and returned in a prepaid envelope for commercial purposes.

Dear Sir / Madam, as far as I know, no one forced you to do this, sorry to write this but the fault lies with you, my client is not responsible for this negligence.

And since 2016 my client has honored the requested advertising service:

Internet link.

From now on, if I have no proposal from you, I inform you that the file will be sent to the bailiff on Monday July 30, 2018 to collect this claim.

Your fanciful threats don't scare me.

Regards,

Mrs. Z,

PAY YOUR INVOICES !!!

If you prefer to pay directly to the bailiff I give you his contact details as well as a payment agreement / contract termination.

Regards,

Not paying is a scam, we have never communicated in this directory!

Thank you

Mrs. Z,

Are you associating my origins with a scam?

I ask you to be very careful with these kinds of allusions and take this matter seriously.

This contract was sent by post, you have read, signed with the stamp of the company and then returned in a pre-paid envelope for commercial purposes.

Ms. Z, no one forced you to do this, I'm sorry to tell you that, but the fault is yours. My client doesn't have to be penalized for this.

You have had an advertising showcase since 2016:

Internet link.

It is normal for my client to be paid for this work.

These invoices must be paid, Madame Z.

If you accept, I will have you establish a payment / contract termination agreement in order to close this file by mutual agreement.

Regards,

Hello,

I'm sorry that this email has reached you, it is indeed a mistake.
I'm in no way trying to associate your name with a scam, far from my intention.

I simply reconcile a potential contract signed with your invoices.

Can you bring me the proof of our subscription because in my opinion we have in no case subscribed to this type of visibility and do not in any way wish to be associated with it.

Mrs. Z,

Did you read my email with the file?

You signed this order form yourself!

Here is the complete file again.

At the risk of repeating myself, here is the active link again since 2016:

Internet link

I will have you establish a payment agreement / contract termination in order to close this file by mutual agreement.

For info this contract is tacit renewal, my client wishes to terminate it after the payment of the first 2 years.

If you refuse to settle these invoices, it is your right and I respect it, the file will be sent to the bailiff at the end of this week.

I await your news !

Regards,

CASE N°35

Hello sir,

Actually I did not see what it was, given that we were not late in our payments, so I understand better, my replacement fell into the trap !!

I therefore forward this file to our legal department who will come back to you.

Regards,

Dear,

I have not received any news from you for this unpaid invoice (File sent by email on April 23, 2018).

You have read my emails and you persist in your silence, this attitude shows that you are guilty and without valid arguments on this matter.

You have abused the trust of my client by not respecting the contract that you have read and signed.

At the request of my client, I ask you one last time to settle this claim!

I am the mediator between you and my client.

If we do not find an amicable solution this week, your file will be sent to the office of bailiffs early next week.

Maybe you prefer to settle these invoices directly to the bailiff ???

Failure to pay this amount within the stipulated time will immediately result in necessary legal action against your business for the original amount plus interest, collection costs, court fees, attorney fees and expenses. In accordance with the terms of the contract, the competent court is the Court of Justice of JUPITER, the applicable law is that of VENUS.

We are required to inform you that this legal action does not require the legal consent or the presence of your company and that the case will be decided solely on the basis of the evidence provided by the claimant which gives rise to a payment mandate. by default. The judgment will be executed in accordance with international regulations to which your country is also bound, in particular the international convention on the recognition and enforcement of foreign judgments in civil and commercial matters and the international convention on choice of court agreements.

We are also required to inform you that on the basis of similar international conflicts, we can estimate your final disbursement, including late fees, court fees and legal fees, between Euro 12,000.00 and Euro 15,000.00.

Regards,

Hello sir,

I am Mrs Y's replacement, can you tell me what invoice it is?

Thank you in advance.

Regards,

Dear,

Since the amicable confrontation with our Cabinet of judicial officers failed:

I would like to inform you that our client XYZ. will sue you in PLUTON at the court of JUPITER to assert your rights.

We are required to inform you that this legal action does not require the legal consent or the presence of your company and that the case will be decided solely on the basis of the evidence provided by the claimant which gives rise to a payment mandate. by default. The judgment will be executed in accordance with international regulations to which your country is also bound, in particular the international convention on the recognition and enforcement of foreign judgments in civil and commercial matters and the international convention on choice of court agreements.

I remind you that this contract is of tacit renewal, if you wish to terminate it officially I am at your disposal.

Being your mediator / negotiator I keep your file until July 31, 2019.

Without response from you, my client will initiate legal proceedings.

Regards,

CASE N°36

Sir,

This case is a scam.
This contract never existed and the invoices are fictitious.
I am completely insensitive to your intimidation.
You can now assign the company XYZ. This will be the occasion for this scam to be tried and to ask for very heavy sanctions against the perpetrators of this scam.

I have no limits on the lawyers I can mandate to get the truth out.

X
Proxy

Mister X,

Thank-you for your prompt response.

Are you associating my origins with a scam?

My work is certainly hated but honest.

I am in contact with you to close this file by mutual agreement, so I ask you a little serious.

I would like to remind you of these important facts:

This order form with cover letter was sent by publi postage (postal mail).

Mr. Z read this order form, then signed with the company stamp and returned in a prepaid envelope for commercial purposes.

Mr. X as far as I know, no one forced Mr. Z to do this, sorry to write this but the fault lies with him, my client is not responsible for this negligence.

And since 2016 my client has honored the requested advertising service:

Internet link.

You can take all the lawyers you want, it's not my problem, it's your money not mine.

So Mister X, what do we do now?

Do we find a suitable solution for both parties to close this file by mutual agreement or do you prefer to go through the legal route, spend money and time ???

If you prefer to pay directly to the bailiff I give you his contact details as well as a payment agreement / contract termination.

Regards,
           CASE N°37
Mister X,

I await your news for this unpaid invoice.
I am the mediator between you and my client.
Regards,

Hello,
What unpaid ???
What customer ???
Cordially.
Mr. X

Hello,

I see very well, no order from me has been made and I am the only person empowered to make this type of decision.
cordially
M.X

Mister X,

You or someone in your company has signed this order form with the stamp of the company which legally commits you.

As you do not want to negotiate this claim and you are in bad faith, your file will be sent to the bailiff on Monday July 16 to recover this claim with the consequences that this entails for your company.

Regards,

Hello,

Thank you for sending me the proof of our company's commitment.

cordially
M.X

Mister X,

I sent you the file by email on July 12 that you have read, the order form is attached to it, just read it again.

FYI I no longer have your file, it is on the desk of my Director who will send it to the bailiff Monday July 16.

If you change your mind today, I will have you draw up a payment / contract termination agreement valid only today to close this file out of court.

Otherwise no need to answer me.

Regards,

Mister X,

I tried twice to call you and they hang up on me.

This unprofessional attitude on your part is not going to erase the bills.

Today is the last to pay your bills, after I send your file to the bailiff to collect this debt with legal proceedings.

Regards,

My direct number: 00.00.00.00.00, please call me as soon as possible.
I have no time to waste with you.
cordially

Hello Mister X,

It's perfect, it's exactly the same thing on my side, no time to waste with you!

Please find attached the payment agreement / termination of contract to return to me (as soon as possible so that I can block your file and avoid you the bailiff) signed with the stamp of your company if you wish to close this file by amicable way.

Once signed, I will send it to my client who will do the same and I will return it to you.

In the subject of the settlement put only the file number so that our accounting department can quickly identify the payment:

000000

If you refuse to settle this claim, it is your right and I respect it.

In this case I will be forced to send your file to the bailiff no later than July 20, 2018.

No more additional time will be granted!

Regards,

CASE N°38

Mister X,

PAY YOUR INVOICES !!!

If you prefer to pay directly to the bailiff I give you his contact details as well as a payment agreement / contract termination.

Regards,

Sir,

I inform you that a complaint to the public prosecutor has been filed and that the investigation is underway.

Please contact the police station of NOUNOU and inform your bailiff.

A report from the General Direction of the National Police was drawn up on May 25, 2018.

Greetings.

Hello Mister X,

Are you associating my origins with something illegal?

If you continue in this direction, I will contact today 2 organizations that you have in CORRUPTLAND to file a complaint against you for discrimination in first and last name.

Are you complaining for not paying your bills?

In short the criminal being dissociated from the commercial, this will not erase the invoices.
And after 30 days, the file will be closed without further action.

By filing a complaint for X reasons, you will be making a false statement.

If you have complained, please be so kind as to send me a copy so that I can add it to your file.

So if you refuse to settle these invoices out of court, I will send your file to the bailiff in order to collect this claim.

And if you have complained to the Police, you will be prosecuted for false declaration, the bailiff is a ministerial officer and will not give you any gifts.

It seems that for this file, you do not have all the elements in hand or else the reality was hidden from you.

Regards,

Sir,

We kindly ask you to find attached an extract of our complaint against the ABCD Company.

Wishing you good reception,

Accept our best regards.

Mister X,

Why did you make a false scam statement?

I would like to remind you of these important facts:

- This contract was sent by publi postage (postal mail).

Mrs. YY read, then signed with the stamp of the company this order form then returned in a pre-franked envelope for commercial purpose.

No one forced Ms. YY to do this.

Sorry to tell you that but the fault lies with him, my client is not responsible for this negligence.

Since 2016, my client has honored his still active advertising service:

Internet link.

To date the scam is on your side because the bills have not been paid.

Mr. X, if we do not find an amicable solution today, I will be forced to transmit your file to the bailiff including this fanciful complaint.

You should understand that the bailiff will contact the police and explain the situation and afterwards you will be prosecuted for making a false statement in order to avoid paying your bills.

Now I'm waiting for an answer from you.

Regards,

CASE N°39

Hello sir,

Well received. This invoice follows an attempted scam from XYZ. Our partners are currently suing her.

So thank you for stopping to contact me about this. I would also add that defending the interests of this organization greatly damages your image.

Good evening,

Mr. X

Mister X,

No attempt to scam from my client.

I am in contact with you to close this file by mutual agreement, so I ask you a little serious.

I would like to remind you of these important facts:

This order form with cover letter was sent by publi postage (postal mail).

This purchase order was read, then signed and returned in a pre-paid envelope for commercial purposes.

Mr. X as far as I know, no one forced Mr. Y to do this, sorry to write this but the fault lies with him, my client is not responsible for this negligence.

And since 2016 my client has honored the requested advertising service:

Internet link.

Do we find a suitable solution for both parties to close this file by mutual agreement or do you prefer to go through the legal route, spend money and time ???

If you prefer to pay directly to the bailiff I give you his contact details as well as a payment agreement / contract termination.

Regards,

CASE N°40

Sir,

You send us a summons for litigation with the company XYZ which does not concern our organization;

It concerns the association PLUTON VENUS;
Information taken, this association has never ordered any service from XYZ;

Information sent to the organizers of the HUHUHU Exhibition is believed to be at the origin of the request and incorrect invoices from XYZ;

A registered letter sent in 2016 to this company reported the error and requested the total cancellation of any business relationship.

Your procedures must therefore now be sent by registered mail to the president of PLUTON VENUS. To your mail should be attached:
- Proof of receipt of your reminders,
- Purchase orders which could have come from PLUTON VENUS, signed by the president of the time, the only authority empowered to act financially for the Organization.

President
M.ZZ

Dear,

We send the file only by email or fax.

By postal mail, the bailiff will take care of it!

Additional costs will be expected.

I can send your file today to the bailiff.
Does this suit you?

Regards,

CASE N°41

Mister Z.

Your Documents are false and the so-called order form and your so-called page on the Internet were stolen from XYZ during the CUCULAND trade fair. You call from PLUTON - your bank is domiciled in VENUSLAND and your letters are on a JUPITER document and arrive from PLOUCLAND!
I am filing a complaint with the CORRUPTLAND police.

Mister X,

Are you associating my origins with something illegal?

I ask you to be very careful with what you write because I can also file a complaint with 2 organizations that you have in CORRUPTLAND.

My work is certainly hated but honest.

I am in contact with you to close this file by mutual agreement, so I ask you a little serious.

I would like to remind you of these important facts:

This order form with cover letter was sent by publi postage (postal mail).

You have read this order form, then signed and returned in a prepaid envelope for commercial purposes.

Mr. X as far as I know, no one forced you to do this, sorry to write this but the fault lies with you, my client is not responsible for this negligence.

And since 2016 my client has honored the requested advertising service:

Internet link.

Mr. X, you have bills to pay and your fraudulent schemes to try to evade your moral obligations will be in vain.

Do we find a suitable solution for both parties to close this file by mutual agreement or do you prefer to go through the legal route, spend money and time ???

And if you have complained for X reasons, the bailiff will sue you for false declaration in order not to pay your bills.

If you prefer to pay directly to the bailiff I give you his contact details as well as a payment agreement / contract termination.

Regards,

Sorry but in principle the letters are addressed to the signatory of the received mail.
And you are well sir
Z
Senior Credit Manage

As stated in the email you sent me.
I did not make any association
Cordially.

CASE N°42

Someone else scammed

thank you

Mister X,

Are you associating my origins with a scam?

I ask you to be very careful with these kinds of allusions and take this matter seriously.

You have invoices to pay Mr. X.

Thanks for doing what's needed !

Regards,

I called the RORO salon which confirms that we are up to date with them.

We called without success

Give me a phone where I can reach you

Mister X,
The "RORO lounge" is not my client.

If you read my 1st email carefully, you can read that my client is XYZ, it is also indicated on the contract that you signed.

Regards,

In object is written RORO lounge

What is XYZ

And who corresponds to what
Give me a phone I call you !!!!!!

Mister X,

Why don't you read the entire package I sent you?

You have all the answers!

Take the time to read the presentation page, everything is indicated!

You can contact me at the phone number below.

Regards,

hi Z
what number can i reach you

Inspector ZZZ

Mister X,

Apparently you are not taking this matter seriously for unpaid invoices.

You use the ABCD logo without their authorization for a possible intimidation on your part against me.

You also use a person's name, false and use of false.

But strangely, you have no arguments to defend yourself.

All you need to do is insult me and the cup is full as you say in CORRUPTLAND.

Mr. X, when will you understand that all this will backfire on you when the bailiff has the file in his hands.

You have the phone number just below and I want to warn you that our conversations may be saved as AVI files by our servers.

The stamp of your company binds you legally.

You will have to pay these bills.

Regards,

The logos are in your email!

Telephone number is not secure on CORRUPTLAND's network
I have contacted the RORO show which confirms that you do not exist and above all we were not present this year!
The manufacturing of a tampon is possible in any supply store
Garage spelling is wrong
Also send me a document that takes your good faith
So I ask you to stop your manipulation otherwise I would do the necessary with the real police service

In your ass Z

Mister X,

For your insult, I expected more, you disappoint me!

Do you want to file a complaint?
What purpose ?

So as not to pay your bills?

I would like to remind you that this order form was sent by publi postage by my client.

You have received it, signed it and returned it in a postage-paid envelope for commercial purposes.

Once your complaint is filed, please be so kind as to send me a duplicate so that it can be added to your file.

You should also know that if you file a complaint, you will make a false declaration and you will be condemned for that and the bailiff will not give you any gifts.

The company "Salon du RORO" acts of unfair competition.

Mr. X you have contractual obligations to keep, you must pay these invoices !!!

MAY BE YOU PREFER TO PAY THESE INVOICES DIRECTLY TO THE OWNER ????

Regards,

I love TUTU Monsieur Z
I was there last week
I explain to you
You think I'm going to make a transfer on a rib at TUTU to a company that is clearly a scam
Did you take me for a truffle?
Stop Please

Mister X,

Why are you tu?

The photo is not suitable for the file!

I am always correct towards you!

But what scam are you talking about?

Why are you absolutely trying to shirk your contractual obligations to my client!?!?

I would like to remind you that since 2016 you have had an advertising showcase for your company and it is quite normal that my client is paid for it.

In the current situation it is YOU who is the scammer, you created this situation yourself.

Mister X I will stop once these invoices are paid or do you want to pay directly to the usher in CORRPUTLAND ???

Regards,

peace Z

crazy peace

Mister X,

You must understand that the Internet is not an authority!

Take this very simple example:

- If one of your competitors accuses you for X reasons on forums!
- Should I believe it ???

You should also understand that I am not harassing you, I contact you during office hours.

I am the mediator between you and my client, my job certainly hated but honest is to avoid you the legal proceedings by bailiff.

So since you want peace, you have a choice:

-Either we find an amicable solution, a possible negotiation of the debt.
-Either you pay directly to the bailiff, additional fees will be added.

I am waiting for your answer.

Regards,

You're heavy Z
Internet is not authority
And you you are nothing in his exchanges
So change pigeon

Mister X,

You never answer my questions for lack of arguments and also in bad faith!

I know that the fact that I am RRR bothers you and moreover I ask you to pay your bills; it's even more painful to admit that.

It is however very simple, you have invoices to pay, pay them to our collection office or to the bailiff!

What do you choose?

RRR?
What is delirium ?
Are you calling me a racist?

I ask you to change pigeon
It is however simple

I just found the block this correspondent tab
Very good !!
For ever

Mister X,

I'm not treating you at all!

You just don't have a clear conscience!

No matter the skin color, we are all of the same breed:

-   Humans

You see you use words that have no meaning.

You must pay these invoices Mr. X today or I will send the file to the bailiff tomorrow morning.

Regards,

Mister X,

Hereby,

I confirm that your file has been sent to our office of bailiffs to recover this debt.

Additional costs will be expected.

It is very unfortunate that you have refused my help on this matter.

Good luck to you for the future.

Regards,

CASE N°43

Hello,

I have already answered this request.

We have terminated our contract, as provided for by the withdrawal law (article L 121-16 and 121-20 of the Consumer Code).

Please stop sending us the warnings. We will not pay this invoice because the contract is invalid. For any additional consultations, please contact our lawyer Mr. Z. Law firm ZZZ.

Regards,

Hello Mister X,

Thank-you for your prompt response.

The termination of the contract had to arrive at my client 12 days at the latest, it is indicated on the contract that I sent to you.

As the contract is VENUSIAN law, your CORRUPTLAND articles do not apply.

You have had an advertising showcase since 2016 and it is quite normal that my client was paid for the work accomplished.

My job is debt collection, so I ask that you settle these invoices as soon as possible.

Being the mediator between you and my client, I am in contact with you to find an amicable solution and avoid you the confrontation with the judicial officer.

Regards,

Hello again,

Yes, I understand, but there is nothing to justify the request of this fraudulent company. The order form from us was signed by a secretary who has no authorization to represent the company. In addition, we immediately terminate this "order". We did everything once to avoid problems.

We know XYZ well; this is not the first time that they have tried something like this with us and with our colleagues. They are well known. Their 'trade' is fraudulent behavior. And after a discussion with our lawyers, we are ready to defend ourselves in court.

Regards,

Mister X,

I understand your dissatisfaction but let me clarify things on certain points.

My client is not a fraudulent company, on the internet we read everything and the truth is not what you might think my client is the victim of unfair competition and defamation.

Take this very simple example:

If one of your competitors puts it on the Internet you are an unreliable company! Should I believe it?

The Internet is not an authority to define what is a fraudulent company, and the Internet or another company does not have to tell you not to pay your bills. Because this case is akin to incitement to crime, punishable as a crime.

This contract was sent by post, Mr. XZ read it, signed with the stamp of the company and then returned in a pre-franked envelope for commercial purposes.

Mr. X, no one forced Mr. XZ to do this, I'm sorry to tell you that, but the fault lies with him.
My client doesn't have to be penalized for this.

Today I have taken your comments into account and with your agreement if you wish I am ready to negotiate this claim with my Director of Cabinet in order to limit the costs for the 2 parties.

If you accept, I will have you establish a payment / contract termination agreement in order to close this file by mutual agreement.

Regards,

Hello,

I will not pay the amount requested. I guarantee that. Thank you for seeing with your client and come back to me with a solution.

Regards,

Mister X,

After hearing from my Chief of Staff, I was able to reduce your claim.

Please find attached the payment agreement / termination of contract to return to me (as soon as possible so that I can block your file and avoid you the bailiff) signed with the stamp of your company if you wish to close this file by amicable way.

Once signed, I will send it to my client who will do the same and I will return it to you.

In the subject of the settlement put only the file number so that our accounting department can quickly identify the payment:

000000

If you refuse to settle this claim, it is your right and I respect it.

In this case I will be forced to send your file to the bailiff no later than June 21, 2018.

Regards,

Hello,

It is done. I am waiting for this signed agreement from you. I made the transfer this morning.

Regards,

Hello Mister X,

Thank you for this signed payment / termination agreement!

I pass it on to my client so that they can sign it too!

Due to the time difference, I will certainly receive it at the end of the day or tomorrow morning at the latest when I take my service.

I will come back to you tomorrow morning and I will also confirm the payment received.

Regards,

CASE N°44

Hello Mr. Z,

I protest purchase order, and invoices from XYZ.
I have never asked this agency for any purpose whatsoever. I regularly participate in the ABCDE congress, and I have never asked for any paid advertising whatsoever. I consider that I have no past relationship with this agency. My website is indeed public and free to access.
Please, Mr. Z, be so kind as to remove me from your databases and to cease all further proceedings and reminders on this matter.

Regards,
Mrs. Y.

Mrs. Y,

Thank-you for your prompt response.

Let me remind you of these facts:

This order form with cover letter was sent by publi postage (postal mail).

This purchase order was read, then signed with the stamp of the company and returned in a prepaid envelope for commercial purposes.

Madam Y as far as I know, no one forced you to do this, sorry to write this but the fault lies with you, my client is not responsible for this negligence.

The cover letter clearly explained the commercial offer, you should have read this letter in full as well as the order form.

And since 2016 my client has honored the requested advertising service:

Internet link.

If you wish to close this file and terminate the tacit renewal contract, you can contact me by email and I will have you establish a payment agreement / contract termination.

From now on, if I have no proposal from you, I inform you that the file will be sent to the bailiff on Monday July 30, 2018 to recover this claim with legal proceedings.

Regards,

Hello Mr. Z,
Here is a copy of this message to the organizers of the ABCDE congress.
Following your summons today, ordering me to pay you an amount of several thousand euros, for BLAHBLAH as described in the messages dated below:

I recognize my signature and the veracity of the information completed on the document labeled ABCDE, according to you "order form".

However, I have never subscribed to any commercial offer from this XYZ agency. My website is public and free to access.

The lawyer contacted for advice, following one of your reminders by post, in February 2017, having confirmed to me on this date a scam, left it is true without prosecution on my side.

I reiterate that you consider having no past relationship with the agency XYZet I beg you, Mr. Z, to be so kind as to withdraw me from your databases, by termination if you wish, and to cease all proceedings or raise about it.

Regards,
Mrs. Y.

Mrs. Y,

This lawyer does not have the right to say that it is a scam because no judgment has been rendered.

So if today we do not find an amicable solution to close this claim, your file will be sent to our office of bailiffs to recover this claim with legal proceedings.

Assume what you have signed and read a document completely before signing it.

Regards,

Mister Z,

Following the telephone call, which you addressed to me this morning and which you voluntarily interrupted after your statement, informing me of your wish today to send the file to a bailiff, I would like to report back to your remark concerning the obligation of payment of invoices for companies, that to pass a convention form for an order form is a crime.

Regards,
Mrs. Y.

Mrs. Y,

Since you refuse to settle these invoices out of court,
I would like to inform you that our client XYZ. will sue you on JUPITER in VENUS court to assert your rights.

The amount claimed will be 3 years (5000, 00 EUROS + recovery costs) as written on the contract that you have read and signed.

We are required to inform you that this legal action does not require the legal consent or the presence of your company and that the case will be decided solely on the basis of the evidence provided by the claimant which gives rise to a payment mandate. by default. The judgment will be executed in accordance with international regulations to which your country is also bound, in particular the international convention on the recognition and enforcement of foreign judgments in civil and commercial matters and the international convention on choice of court agreements.

We are also required to inform you that on the basis of similar international conflicts, we can estimate your final disbursement, including late fees, court fees and legal fees, between Euro 12,000.00 and Euro 15,000.00.

Regards,

Hello Mr. ZZ,

I acknowledge receipt of your email today.
Mr. YY, in copy of this message, President of ABCDE is in charge of this file.

Regards,
Mrs. Y.
chairwoman

Hello Mrs. Y,

It's heard !

I forgot to tell you that I keep your file until September 27, 2018.

Regards,

Hello Sir, it is an error I paid XYZ for the rental of a location at the ZZ show in November 2015 if I remember correctly but I deny asking them to make advertisements outside the congress, and in no European country .
It is absolutely necessary to settle this dispute and that the company "XYZ clarifies things because I will not pay.
PS I also send this message to Y who also takes care of the XYZ congress in PUTLAND, I have participated three times already. And jzmzis I was not informed of this practice which I consider as fraudulent.
Hello Mister X,

Did you read my email correctly?

My client is ZZZ.

XYZ I don't know!

Read again what I sent you!

Do you refuse to pay these bills?

No worries, I send the file today at the end of the day to the bailiff to recover this debt with legal proceedings.

Sorry, but I have no time to waste.

Read what you sign dear Mr. X.

I await your confirmation for the transmission of your file to the bailiff.

Regards,

Hello sir yes I refuse. It all smells like a scam. And are you calling him this morning from a number at BOULAND? I'm only dealing with XYZ for congresses, they never asked for me.
Forward to the court I do the same by the lawyer for improper prosecution. I will not let go of anything be certain I know the subject well.
See you later

Mister X,

Sorry but there are no scams!

You have created this situation yourself by not fully reading this order form.
The fault lies with you, my client does not have to be penalized for your negligence.

Take all the avocados you want, it's your money not mine.

I'm calling from BOULAND (European Union) and then what's the problem?
You are in CORRUPTLAND and you are a person who refuses to pay his bills

Since you refuse to pay these invoices and to terminate this contract with tacit agreement, I therefore transmit your file to the bailiff tomorrow morning to recover this claim with legal proceedings.

I was in contact with you to negotiate this claim but you refuse my help, too bad for you.

Regards,

Mister X,

You have 4 weeks to provide us with the contact details of your lawyer who will represent you at the JUPITER Commercial Court.
Your lawyer must have a license to practice on JUPITER and practice SSSSSSSSS fluently.

Regards,

CASE N°46

Hello sir,

Thank you for these different documents and for your email.

As you can see from the links below: "XYZ" and your client are not receiving good press and are even considered a scam.
Internet link
Internet link
Internet link
Internet link

At the legal level now, the order formulated does not constitute a valid contract despite the small lines inserted at the bottom of the page.
In addition, the invoices are not in the name of XYZ but of ZZZ not specified in "the order form" and are not due.

Finally following your email, I therefore think of filing a handrail with the authorities and will send you a copy of it.

Yours,

Hello,

In addition, the following registered letter was sent - by registered mail - to your customer denouncing the order form at the end of 2016.

Yours,

Dear Mr. X,

Thank-you for your prompt response.

The termination letter arrived too late, as the contract had to be terminated 12 days after the date of signing.

I did not know that in CORRUPTLAND a company pays its invoices according to what is written on the Internet.

The Internet is not an authority to define what is a scam.

Do you want to file a complaint?

What is the purpose of not paying the bills?

The commercial being dissociated from the criminal, this will not erase the invoices and making a false declaration will backfire on you when the bailiff will have the file if you refuse to settle this claim out of court.

My client is a victim of defamation and unfair competition.

If I read slanderous articles about your company on the internet, should I believe them?

Let me remind you of these facts:

This order form with cover letter was sent by publi postage (postal mail).

This purchase order was read, then signed with the stamp of the company and returned in a prepaid envelope for commercial purposes.

Mr. X as far as I know, no one forced Ms. Y to do this, sorry to write this but the fault lies with him, my client is not responsible for this negligence.

And since 2016 my client has honored the requested advertising service:

Internet link.

Today I am in contact with you to close this file by mutual agreement, being the mediator between the company ZZZ and my client XYZ, I remain at your disposal if you have a proposal for me.

The 3rd year will be invoiced in a few months and my client wishes to be paid for the 2 years or a part and especially to terminate this tacit renewal contract.

Awaiting your response.

Regards,

Hello Mr. Z,

Out of curiosity, where are you based?

Mister X
COO

Hello Mister X,

Our collections office is located in BOULAND (European Union).

Regards,

Hello,

To come back to simple and factual things, we do not consider this purchase order as valid because the signatory of the "purchase order" was made by our accountant who is not authorized to sign purchase orders and that the company stamp has no legal value.
In addition, concerning the assignment of receivables, it is written that you have the power of attorney for the company "XYZ" based in KILLAND but we have no commitment towards this company, the order form being in the name of XYZ based in ORION.

Mister X,

It does not matter who signed this order because the company is responsible for its employees.

The stamp legally commits the company.

Finally, know that I have been doing this job for a very long time and that I know all the "tricks" of debtors to not pay the bills.

Attached is the official document of the transfer of the company to my client's KILLAND.

In order not to waste time, I keep your file until Friday, July 27, 2018.

Regards,

We will not hesitate to file a complaint for fraud in the event of a prosecution.

The next contacts will be made through our lawyer.

Yours

Mister X,

But what scam are you talking about?

Do you have an official link where my client was sentenced for X reasons?

I do a hated but honest job.

Take a lawyer if you wish but once again the invoices will not be erased and the contract not terminated.
And you will start spending money!

As I had in my previous email, I have been doing this job for a very long time and threats no longer scare me.

Since the start of our email exchanges I have never had a moment of good faith from you at any time, I have just had fanciful threats from you of future complaints.

For each file that I treat, I analyze it and put myself in the "2 camps" if I can express myself thus.

gentlemen,
Is it so difficult to admit that Madame Y signed this purchase order without having read it in full?
The cover letter explained the commercial offer well.

Again and sorry to write it again but the fault lies with him.

From now on, if I have no proposal from you, I inform you that the file will be sent to the bailiff on Monday July 30, 2018 to collect this claim.

Regards,

We are talking about you of course
 Internet link .

We will be vigilantly following the advice of our Gendarmes friends:

Mister X
COO

Dear,

Since you refuse to settle these invoices out of court,

I would like to inform you that our client XYZ. will sue you on JUPITER in VENUS court to assert your rights.

The amount claimed will be 3 years (6,000.00 EUROS + recovery costs) as written on the contract that you have read and signed.

We are required to inform you that this legal action does not require the legal consent or the presence of your company and that the case will be decided solely on the basis of the evidence provided by the claimant which gives rise to a payment mandate. by default. The judgment will be executed in accordance with international regulations to which your country is also bound, in particular the international convention on the recognition and enforcement of foreign judgments in civil and commercial matters and the international convention on choice of court agreements.

We are also required to inform you that on the basis of similar international conflicts, we can estimate your final disbursement, including late fees, court fees and legal fees, between Euro 12,000.00 and Euro 15,000.00.

Regards,

CASE N°47

Mister X,

PAY YOUR INVOICES !!!

If you prefer to pay directly to the bailiff I give you his contact details as well as a payment agreement / contract termination.

Regards,

 Screw you !!

Mister X,

Thank you for your responsiveness but when the insults rain, your arguments are non-existent for this claim.

You have to understand that I do my collection work, you have bills to pay!

You have the choice, settle these invoices at our collection office or directly at the bailiff!

I will have you establish a payment / contract termination agreement at your request.

Mister X, you have to assume what you signed, that's all!

To have "peace" as you say, you have to pay these bills because after the bailiff will put even more pressure on you.

Regards,

You are really charlots, your methods work?

Mister X,

A little serious, please!

You have bills to pay!

Maybe you prefer to pay them directly to the bailiff,

Regards,

Please send me the police too,

It is already done, 10d ago

Mister X,

You mix everything!

Invoices must be paid either to our collections office or to the office of bailiffs.

The Police are not empowered to collect debts.

And I specify that this contract is tacit renewal, it must also be terminated and at the same time pay these 2 invoices.

On this order form that you signed with the stamp of the company, you have legally committed your company.

Why do you refuse to assume your responsibilities as a business manager?

Again, if you prefer to settle directly with the bailiff I give you his contact details as well as a payment agreement / contract termination.

I am waiting for your answer.

Regards,

, funny

CASE N°48

Mister X,

You have read my email with the file for this unpaid invoice but no response from you.

Your silence will only make the situation worse.

PAY YOUR INVOICES !!!

If you prefer to pay directly to the bailiff I give you his contact details as well as a payment agreement / contract termination.

I keep your file until August 06, 2018.

Regards,

Hello,
You have the nerve to tell me to pay your bills. Knowing that it comes from a scam! I have a file on the progress of this case. I ask you to remove me from your lists, and to stop writing to me.
Otherwise we will complete the file with harassment.
Sir, I don't salute you.
Regards,

Hello Mister X,

Thank-you for your prompt response.

Sorry but there is no harassment on my part, I am contacting you regarding unpaid invoices and the 2 emails you received were sent during office hours.

No scams and I ask you to have a slightly more responsible attitude to this matter.

Let me remind you of these facts:

This order form with cover letter was sent by publi postage (postal mail).

This purchase order was read, then signed with the stamp of the company and returned in a prepaid envelope for commercial purposes.

Mr. X as far as I know, no one forced you to do this, sorry to write this but the fault lies with you, my client is not responsible for this negligence.

The cover letter clearly explained the commercial offer, Mr. X you should have read this letter in full as well as the order form.

And since 2016 my client has honored the requested advertising service:

Internet link.

If you wish to close this file and terminate the tacit agreement, I will have you establish a payment agreement / contract termination.

From now on, if I have no proposal from you, I inform you that the file will be sent to the bailiff Wednesday August 08, 2018 to recover this claim.

Being the mediator between you and my client, I remain open to all negotiations on your part.

CASE N°49

Dear Z,

We have been stalked by **XYZ**
This is a **SCAM company** and we don't know anything about this!
We don't know what your role is here, if you are part of the scam or not (hopefully you are an honest man).

We don't know the signature on the attached "bon de commande", they can't give us more information, we didn't ordered anything with them.
We have send a registered letter (attachment) in the summer of 2017, to tell them we don't know anything about it and they are a scam company.

But just to make clear, we don't KNOW anything about this, won't PAY anything and really want to STOP this!

Met vriendelijke groeten
Kind regards

Dear Y,

Your email is scandalous !

You associate my name Z as a scam.

I will contact this organization against racism in your country :

Lien Internet

I know my job is not so popular but my job is honest.

For memory :

This order form was sent by mail to your company.
Somebody of ZZZ read this order form , sign and after put in prepaid envelope for sending.

You have to ask who sign this contract in your company.

If your director don't want to pay these invoices, I will send the file to bailiff for legal pursuit including your name and surname because you associate my name Z as a scam.

If your director wants pay, I will send a letter agreement with cancellation of contract.

I keep the file until Friday 03 August 2018.

Regards

Dear Z,

I didn't say that you are a scam, I'm telling you that the company **XYZ.,** who hired your services is a scam!
Since we are an international company, we work a lot with foreign people, and I assure you that I'm not a racist.

I have colleagues that do the same job as you, and I'm amazed by their talent and patience.
So let us please be clear that I don't despise you in any way.

As for the order. Can you send me the **mail** where the order was filed?
Surely XYZ should be able to provide this to us…

I've asked everyone in the Conference company about this. Nobody knows anything. You can't provide us with a name, you only have the name of our company and a signature that, let us be fair, a five year old child could have drawn.

To conclusion, I'm not a racist, we hold XYZ responsible for being a SCAM, not you and we won't pay anything we didn't order.

Y,

Advise your Direction about this file !

I will send the file to bailiff Friday 03 August 2018.

Regards.

Dear Z,

I can only inform you that our directory advises us to be aware of SCAM companies and tells us to don't pay anything that we didn't order.

I'm sorry if that makes your job difficult, but we didn't order anything. XYZ is a SCAM, so we won't pay anything.
Please contact XYZ about this, we can't do anything more.

Met vriendelijke groeten
Kind regards

Y,

If you believe all what you read on Internet......

For example, if I read on Internet the company ZZZ is not so serious and you too !

Is it true or not ?

Who I must believe ?

So you accuse my Client XYZ to be a scam, you are a diffamous person without respect for anybody.

The full exchange of emails will be send to the bailiff Friday 03 August 2018.

And I will contact the same day the ABCD.

Regards.

Z,

If you can **PROVE** that we ordered **anything**, this would be a whole other conversation.

Met vriendelijke groeten
Kind regards

Good morning,

Inform your direction about this debt :

3 days for make the payment.

Regards.

CASE N° 50

Hello,

Upon receipt of the invoice we immediately sent several letters informing that it should be canceled because we did not understand that it was a paid order but just a request for information following our presence at the ABCDE fair.

We never received a response despite our multiple submissions. You will find copies of the letters as an attachment.

We think this is a scam, because any company can be understanding because it can often be wrong. Especially since we did not leave the thing lying around, we immediately sent a letter to cancel the so-called pub.

Could you therefore approach your client to warn him that we have sent them several letters and that in conclusion this will not be honored.

I hope you understand our position.
Best regards.

Hello Mrs. Y,

Thank-you for your prompt response.

Unfortunately the first letter to cancel this contract arrived too late, as stipulated on the contract it was necessary that the letter of denunciation arrives at the latest 12 days after the date of signature of the contract.

In the file, I have indeed your letters that you sent but also the answers of my client !!!

Madam Y, why did you lie to me?
It is a very serious professional misconduct, this important element will be added to the file if it should be sent to the bailiff to recover this claim.

Sorry but there is no scam from my client!

Let me remind you of these facts:

This order form with cover letter was sent by publi postage (postal mail).

This purchase order was read, then signed and returned in a pre-paid envelope for commercial purposes.

Mrs. Y as far as I know, no one forced Mr. XX to do this, sorry to write this but the fault lies with him, my client is not responsible for this negligence.

The cover letter clearly explained the commercial offer, Mr. XX should have read this letter in its entirety as well as the order form.

And since 2016 my client has honored the requested advertising service:

Internet link.

If you wish to close this file and terminate the tacit agreement, I will have you establish a payment agreement / contract termination.

From now on, if I have no proposal from you, I inform you that the file will be sent to the bailiff Tuesday August 07, 2018 to collect this claim.

Being the mediator between you and my client, I remain open to all negotiations on your part.

Sir,

Thanks for your feedback. However, I inform you that we have not received any response from them !!

And even if the deadline was exceeded I think that as a professional they can make an effort and cancel the advertisement. It is called to be of good liver and to be understanding. Especially since we asked to remove the advertisement !! Because we didn't want that, we didn't care.

Any company can make a commercial effort (even the deadline exceeded) especially when the customer responds by mail and explains the error.

At one point the error is human and as mentioned above we acted quickly, upon receipt of the invoice we explained to them that we had not seen that it was chargeable and that it was just a data update.
I do not understand why such relentlessness.

Mrs. Y,

I understand the situation and put myself in your place.

You should understand that since 2016, you have had a showcase on the Internet promoting the company XYZ and it is quite normal that my client is paid for the work performed.

Since you're talking about a business effort, what I can do is talk to my Chief of Staff and reduce your debt.
In this case, it is important that this tacit renewal contract be terminated.

I await your answer to find out if you wish to settle part of the claim.

Otherwise, I will be forced to regretfully forward this file to the bailiff (additional costs will be added by the bailiff) to collect this claim.

Regards,

Hello,

Thanks for your understanding. Please note that it is not in our interest not to pay for a service. We have a very good relationship with all of our suppliers, it's not our kind of not paying.

If we order it is to pay next. We are a company and we know what it represents an unpaid amount.

Thank you for trying to chat with the Director for the commercial gesture and explaining to him what happened, I remain available if he wishes to contact me. Yours sincerely.

Hello Mrs. Y,

After hearing from my Chief of Staff, I was able to reduce your claim.

Please find attached the payment agreement / termination of contract to return to me (as soon as possible so that I can block your file and avoid you the bailiff) signed with the stamp of your company if you wish to close this file by amicable way.

Once signed, I will send it to my client who will do the same and I will return it to you.

In the subject of the settlement put only the file number so that our accounting department can quickly identify the payment:

000000

If you refuse to settle this claim, it is your right and I respect it.

In this case I will be forced to transmit with regret your file to the bailiff no later than August 07, 2018 to recover this claim with legal proceedings.

Regards,

www.ingramcontent.com/pod-product-compliance
Lightning Source LLC
Chambersburg PA
CBHW080458220526
45465CB00006B/2309